FRENCH NOVELISTS OF TODAY

MILTON H. STANSBURY

French

Novelists

of

Today

UNIVERSITY OF PENNSYLVANIA PRESS: PHILADELPHIA

1935

Foreword

IN concentrating on a few of the outstanding figures from the rich and chaotic stream of contemporary French letters, this small volume aspires to present more intimately a restricted number of writers rather than trace a more comprehensive, and therefore colder, panorama. The choice was governed not by the author as artist, but by his representative and colorful personality. This will account for the absence of such brilliant names as Jacques de Lacretelle or Roger Martin du Gard, and for the inclusion in some instances of less talented but more significant men. Although there are probably more American readers of the living French writers than is generally supposed, our knowledge is too often confined to such works as the *Jean-Christophe* of Romain Rolland or the biographies of Maurois. If Julien Green, Romains' *Men of Good Will,* and Céline's *Journey to Night's End* are more familiar to the American public than men like Mauriac, Giraudoux, or MacOrlan, a part of their popularity is attributable to their availability in translated form. Through lack of publicity rather than of merit many of the best contemporary French novelists are neglected in the United States.

In these short essays, I submit my reactions to those living French novelists who have most stimulated my own interest. If in introducing and analyzing a few new personalities I should inspire either curiosity or enthusiasm in their behalf, this alone would justify my book.

M. H. S.

Contents

		PAGE
Foreword		V
CHAPTER		
I.	André Gide	I
II.	Jean Giraudoux	19
III.	François Mauriac	33
IV.	Pierre MacOrlan	53
V.	Valery Larbaud	69
VI.	Paul Morand	83
VII.	Colette	101
VIII.	The Surrealists	121
IX.	Jean Cocteau	137
X.	Julien Green	147
XI.	Henry de Montherlant	157
XII.	Pierre Drieu La Rochelle	175
XIII.	Jules Romains	189
XIV.	André Malraux	209

André Gide

To condense the portrait of André Gide within the dimensions of a single essay is like attempting to crowd into one room the furnishings of an entire house. Obviously some essential piece, some *objet d'art,* must be conspicuous by its absence. As a literary artist, critic, satirist, moralist, compelling personality, and outstanding influence, he plays many rôles, which would require as many chapters. But no matter how selective and incomplete the sketch, Gide's place is first in any gallery of contemporary French novelists. His seniority alone would entitle him to this position, for he has been an active literary figure since the last decade of the nineteenth century, while his youthful spirit ranks him among the most progressive. In 1891 he began discovering life in *Les Cahiers d'André Walter;* today, at the age of sixty-five, he is still discovering it. Never static, aiming not "to be" but "to become," he has ever maintained an open mind. He is a man who has been both loved and feared; hailed as a saint and denounced as a demon. His powerful enemies are only exceeded by his passionate admirers. Groping, vacillating, testing, he has challenged the whole field of conventional ethics. But neither his eccentricities of character nor his heresies have prevented him from being acclaimed one of the foremost writers and thinkers of the present day in France. One of his salient traits is complete non-prejudice of mind. His own irregularity of conduct demanded so much tolerance that to expect mercy, to be logical, he must himself possess an emancipated spirit. If his standard in this respect is almost inaccessibly high, the conscientious reader strives with all the greater earnestness to understand rather than judge this contradictory spirit, so difficult to define and classify. If we believe Henry de Montherlant, the stupid narrow-mindedness of Gide's opponents is a sufficient reason for refusing to be found among their ranks.

"Sometimes it seems to me," writes Gide at the age of fifty-seven, "that I have lived my life inside out and that at the moment of old age my true youth is about to start. My soul made its beginnings covered with wrinkles assiduously traced by my ancestors and my parents, and I had the utmost difficulty in effacing them." These revealing lines from Gide's autobiography, *Si le grain ne meurt,* furnish a key to his entire career, for each of his works marks the systematic rubbing out of some moral wrinkle. If finally he stands reborn and serene, it is only after long, tormented years of hesitation and self-scrutiny. His were not ordinary wrinkles; in fact, the lines traced by his sexual abnormality proved ineradicable. His solution was to beautify his desire so that in his own eyes it should cease to disfigure.

From whatever angle Gide is studied, his memoirs offer the most intelligent point of departure. Although appearing at a comparatively late period in his career, they are indispensable in throwing light on much that would otherwise be obscure in his earlier work. Tracing his life to the age of twenty-five, he holds back nothing and lays bare the problems of these youthful years with frankness and humility. We read of what one outraged critic, Paul Souday, calls his "scabrous" sexual aberrations; we are told how Gide's puritanical upbringing rendered these sexual riddles all the more insoluble; how his conscientious chastity towards women, accepted for a long time as a virtue, obscured the realization that abnormal forms of indulgence were becoming habitual; and we hear Gide's famous cry: "In the name of what God or ideal am I to be forbidden to live according to my nature?"

We see finally his discord resolved into harmony: "I am no longer uneasy in my mind; I have ceased to struggle against my demon; I resist desire no longer."

If Gide was eventually persuaded that he could be accepted as a part of the divine scheme and "that God must hold in horror a uniformity against which even nature protests," the world was not of the same opinion. Society would not accept his plea for individual morals nor his argument that "every intelligent being, every enlightened one at least, has his special rôle to play," and that "every effort to conform to a common rôle is nothing short of treachery." It was due to Gide's physiological twist, due to the world's intolerance of his desires, that his soul as well fell ill. This early struggle was so prolonged that he arrived at the threshold of old age before he attained the inner peace necessary to adjust himself to a hostile universe and view his life with anything approaching equanimity.

This explains the hesitating and contradictory nature of his early work. It accounts for the baffled uncertainty of his critics before 1926 when *Si le grain ne meurt* enlightened them. His readers had probably surmised the nature of his secret long before the official disclosure. It would have been impossible for a man who for thirty years had been writing about handsome Arab boys, vitiated youths, and homosexual husbands, not to have given some inkling of his interests. He had even written *Corydon,* a pseudo-scientific tract in defense of sexual inversion. But it was not until he signed his confessions that anyone was authorized to call Gide himself a Corydon.

Well aware of the equivocal nature of his writings and the cloud hanging over him, he decided on an outspoken revelation. "I have written *Si le grain ne meurt,*" he explains, "to create a precedent, to enlighten some, to reassure others, to force public opinion to take into account that of which it is ignorant—or affects to be ignorant—to the great detriment of psychology, morals, art, and society. I have written it because I prefer to be hated for what I am than loved for what I am not."

These were, in fact, the most extraordinary confessions in all French letters; in comparison with what Gide dared to reveal, the sins of Jean-Jacques Rousseau seemed the merest peccadillos. No longer obliged to whisper innuendos about a man who shouted the truth aloud, the critics were forced to take a stand. Many of the older ones were adamant. They would permit a writer to differ from them on religion, politics, or art; when the sacred code of sex was challenged, they turned a deaf or hostile ear. The inevitable storm of protest greeted Gide's disclosures. Massis, a conservative Catholic, denounced him as demoniacal and subversive. Paul Souday dismissed his sexual aberrations as "mediocre and devoid of interest"; but when the hero of *Les Caves du Vatican* kills his unknown traveling companion, Souday was obviously fascinated by the "Gidian" conception of unmotivated crime. Pierre Lièvre found the subject of sexual inversion repellent and lacking in universal appeal, and denied its legitimacy as literary material. On the other hand, he sanctioned the introduction of the parricide, the traitor, and the incestuous character, arguing that these could be depicted by a truly great master so that the reader discovers in himself the embryonic roots of such sins. He adds: "It would be difficult to imagine a homosexual theme accomplishing the same results. From the very fact that we are men (*homo sum*), how can we be moved or vibrate in common with a subject which is foreign to us?"

Gide's argument was that every sentiment could be found in man, but certain ones had been given the exclusive right to be judged natural, instead of being called simply more frequent, and he adds: "As if the frequent were more natural than the rare, or lead more natural than gold!" Far from considering his physiological peculiarities a virtue, as certain critics had asserted, he contended that homosexuality was only one among more triumphant sins. But it must be admitted that he argues rather arrogantly. He not only strove to prove, as in *Corydon,* that inversion must be a part of nature's plan since it also exists in the lower animals, but he ransacked history to discover examples of famous men who were persecuted on no more logical grounds. In his book on Montaigne, he draws a none too modest comparison between the author of the *Essais* and himself. Had not Montaigne likewise refused to enroll himself under any faction? Were he living now, would he not be undergoing a torment similar to Gide's own? In the same vein is *Numquid et tu,* where Gide points out in certain Gospel verses the analogy between himself and the martyred men of Biblical days. *Numquid et tu* ("Are we not all?") is a proud plea for tolerance: Sinners all, says Gide; therefore, let not his case be singled out for condemnation. *Si le grain ne meurt,* with its straightforward admissions, gained him far greater sympathy and popularity than all his other more devious attempts at vindication. The frank confession of an offense has the curious effect of softening the world's censure. The only unpardonable sin is the unconfessed one, for human nature is so oddly constituted that above all else it resents exclusion. The attitude of Gide's new admirers is expressed by Montherlant: "What annoyed me in Gide's earlier attitude was the suspicious halo he cast over certain feelings through his lack of frankness. It was not until he wrote *Si le grain ne meurt* that I could shake hands with him as man to man."

However, it is doubtful if Gide, with all his courage, would have dared to publish either *Corydon* or *Si le grain ne meurt,* had not Marcel Proust first paved the way. *Corydon,* written thirteen years earlier, was submitted to the public in 1924, three years after the success of *Sodome et Gomorrhe* had proved that the world would not only read, but, in the case of Proust, read with interest, the story of the invert. Largely due to Proust, society was beginning to regard inversion as a pathological rather than a moral issue, and this was already an immense concession and an important step towards tolerance. In reality, Gide was far the braver of the two, for Proust, although he treated all love as a disease, was careful to pose as a heterosexual and portrayed homosexuality chiefly in its abject or comic phases. Gide treated it not as a malady, but as a human problem like any other, and stressed the exaltation and ecstasy of his own inverted loves.

If Gide's autobiography throws light upon his earlier works, they in turn illumine his life. The sum total of experience, he believed, is too complicated for precise expression, and no matter how great the zeal for truth, autobiography can never be more than half sincere. The narrator is obliged to present himself in successive stages, whereas in reality certain phases may very well be simultaneous. Besides, what is sincerity, he asks. Is not concern for this quality to be found "only in those people who have nothing to reveal?" To his mind, sincerity is never of value except when difficult of attainment, and only the banal soul can achieve a completely sincere revelation. He concluded that the novel, which enables its author to be selective, affords greater opportunity than biography for telling the truth. It is a fact that Gide's works of fiction are not less self-revealing than his autobiography. Admitting that there is a potential Gide in each one of his characters, he invites his readers to supply their own interpretation. In the introduction to *Paludes,* he says: "Before explaining my book to others, I am waiting for others to explain it to me. In the first place, any explanation of a book immediately restricts its possibilities, for if the author does not know what he wished to say, how can he know whether he may not have said more than that? What interests me most is what I may have put into a book without realizing it."

In his first book, *Les Cahiers d'André Walter,* written at

the age of twenty, Gide paints his own portrait in the youthful poet André. Ignorant of life, deceived by his puritanical education, he has never declared his love for his cousin Emmanuèle, who dies soon after she marries another man. Thereafter, André's love doubles in intensity. Dreaming of a future reunion of their souls, he feels that death in destroying the barrier of their bodies has only bound them closer. In *La Porte étroite,* written some eighteen years later, it is the heroine who sacrifices her passion for the salvation of her soul, but aside from this reversal of rôles, the hero Jérôme resembles the passive, inert lover of the earlier book. It is difficult to accept at face value this story of the enigmatic and mystical Alissa. Courted by a man who feels for her a chivalrous and platonic friendship only, she senses in him a lack of physical urge. In her fiancé's absence, she experiences the perfectly normal longing of a healthy creature of flesh and blood. What is there in his presence which invariably dispels her desire? What is the subtle detachment which at every meeting renders their love incomplete? "Poor Jérôme!" writes Alissa in her journal. "If he knew that he need make only one gesture and that I am waiting for that gesture!" Although she feels it her Christian duty to sacrifice her earthly love to God, neither Alissa nor Gide makes this renunciation very plausible. The reader of *Si le grain ne meurt* who remembers Gide's own love affair with his cousin, also named Emmanuèle, surmises better than the timid, bewildered Jérôme the real nature of his instincts.

Had Jérôme and Alissa married, their story might have resulted in the situation portrayed in *L'Immoraliste,* an earlier work. Here, in spite of an unconsummated marriage, the husband argues that since he has never loved another woman, it must be his wife he loves. In the course of their travels in North Africa, however, the Arab boys open his eyes to a more sensual urge, an experience resembling Gide's own and termed by Souday his *garçonneries*. Henceforth bored in the company of his wife, Michel indirectly causes her death by selfishly neglecting her health.

If in *Les Cahiers d'André Walter*, the divorce of the soul and body resulted in the poet's death, Gide learned how to live from this very dissociation. He evolved rapidly from the dreamy, melancholy mystic of his early years into the ardent hedonist who, in 1897, wrote *Les Nourritures terrestres*. In this book, which has been called "a breviary of the senses, a hymn to life, beauty, nature, a poem of longing and desire, a call to love," Gide discloses his intense thirst to experience every possible emotion and his apprehension lest a single one escape him. His desire is insatiable. "I am afraid that every longing, every possibility not satisfied in my lifetime will torment me by outliving me. I shall die disconsolate." He found fulfilment inferior to desire, which he cultivated as an end in itself. "Fatigue alone is culpable. Regrets, remorse, repentance, are only yesterday's joys viewed in retrospect." Believing that every perfect action is accompanied by voluptuous physical pleasure, he conceived God as meaning all that one loves or would like to love. "Every form of God is worthy of being cherished, and everything is some form of God. The essential is to find real joy in what we do." In making God synonymous with fervor, in reducing fervor to little more than physical desire, Gide was not inspired by any sort of spiritual aspiration. Nor does he pretend to be, for he says: "Though I am always glad when some doctrine or system of regulated thought seems to justify my acts, I have had to recognize that at times I adopted these doctrines and systems simply as a protection for my sensuality." Unfortunately, in his quest for sensations, Gide found it increasingly difficult to make a choice. Any selection would involve renouncing all the rest, and the prodigious quantity of this 'rest' seemed preferable to any conceivable single unit. His fear of missing any part of life is his argument for holding himself forever unattached, available for anything life might have to offer. But in this surrendering to his instincts, in this constant rebirth of soul and body, his thirst unquenched, the ardent pilgrim of *Les Nourritures terrestres* returns to lament upon the vanity of all things, and throws his book away.

Three or four of Gide's books are presented in the form of light farces, or *soties,* an archaic terminology which he revived to indicate that each character is a *sot.* In one of the earliest of these, *Prométhée mal enchaîné* (1899), Prometheus, or Gide himself, is striving to fathom all he sees in life. The eagle is his temperament or devouring passion. When this passion is neglected, the eagle pines away and dies; to flourish, it must draw its sustenance from the soul. If man can reconcile himself to his passion, he will attain happiness, although this passion will ultimately consume him. If sufficiently nourished, however, it will carry him through and beyond this imprisoning life, and in each one of us, Gide claims, lurks some secret desire which at first appears unworthy. Only by cherishing and cultivating it, can it be transformed into something beautiful, even justifiable. So, in *Prométhée,* a book whose surface gaiety does not conceal the underlying tragedy, Gide has presented in ironical and fanciful manner his own profound problem.

In a later *sotie, Les Caves du Vatican* (1914), a band of swindlers have circulated the report that the Pope is held a prisoner in the Vatican cellars and a false pontiff is masquerading in his place. To investigate this rumor, the grotesque Amédée Fleurissoire, a devout Catholic, departs at once for Italy. He is destined never to return, for sharing his railway compartment is a young adventurer named Lafcadio, the illegitimate son of the Comte de Baraglioul, who to test his doctrine of individual freedom and gratuitous action, decides to hurl the unprepossessing Amédée from the swiftly moving train. This unprovoked crime, and spectacular demonstration of the theory that one's personality should be emancipated and enriched at any cost, is Gide's own thrust at society and all conventional ethics. As a young man who stabs himself in punishment each time he yields to any weakening of the spirit; who through sport rather than pity saves a child from a burning house; who pays another's debts but neglects his own; who, being of illegitimate birth, is an outcast from society and therefore absolved from its laws, Lafcadio is an embodiment of human liberty, and as such, the Gidian hero *par excellence*.

It was not until 1926, at the age of fifty-seven, that Gide was willing to term one of his books—*Les Faux-Monnayeurs*— a novel. Perhaps he felt that this was the first one sufficiently objective to deserve the name. *L'Immoraliste, La Porte étroite, Isabelle, La Symphonie pastorale,* and others, are modestly entitled *récits,* for the story, written in the first person, follows a single thread and reflects the personality of the narrator. Inspired by the Russian novelists, principally Dostoevsky, Gide conceives the novel as an enormous stage where many characters play their parts. Their countless adventures and the interplay of the varied psychological factors are presented so as to convey the complexity of reality. Unwilling to bind himself to any fixed plan of development, he writes the biography of a novel, and depicts the author in the throes of creation, which he interrupts from time to time to assume the rôle of critic. However, in the 'I' of the hero-author may be recognized Gide himself, for he, like Edouard, was tormented by the almost insuperable difficulty of creating living characters instead of constrained and mutilated representations of life. "We are usually taught to admire as good composition," writes Edouard in his notes, "the creation of characters who act consistently throughout in exactly the manner one expects of them. But such a portrait is the very thing which proves that these characters are

artificially created. Life presents at every turn a quantity of
leads for dramas, but it is rare that these develop in the manner
the novelist finds convenient." Confronted with this problem,
Gide explains: "Since the rule of my game is never to profit
from the impulse already acquired, with each new chapter I
feel obliged to set out anew. This makes each new beginning as
arduous as that which perplexed me at the threshold of the
book, and which was the cause of so much lingering hesitation, and days when I despaired of ever again setting my
machine in motion." The author's own uncertainty accounts
for the novel's unsteady rhythm. Constantly alarmed lest he
should fail to present his characters with complete objectivity,
forever plunging afresh into his narrative only to recoil for
retrospective critical examination, continually challenging his
reader and shaking him by the shoulder, Gide infects his audience with his own agitation, and we are never completely easy
in our minds until, with the last page, the author's difficulties
are solved. Despite the elimination of all realistic detail, all
external features and other self-imposed restrictions, Gide suc-
ceeds in creating living characters. Supplied only with their
words and actions, we yet learn to know these people well. In
the gallery of thirty-five portraits which comprise this book
are to be found the most varied forms of human relationships, and
love is viewed from a variety of angles: intellectual, fraternal,
paternal, conjugal, adulterous, and homosexual. You see the
clumsy efforts at happiness of young men and women. There
is a group of school children with their vanities, shams, cruelty,
and corruption. Always young himself, Gide is eminently qualified to trace the lines of demarcation which separate each age.
Elderly people play their part as well, for Gide complains that
the older generation is too rarely mentioned by the modern
novelist. However, in the deplorable old people he chooses to
depict can be seen his fundamental lack of sympathy with old

age. As the title indicates, *Les Faux-Monnayeurs* deals with counterfeiters. Gide's real investigation, however, is not directed towards forged coins, but forged lives, and his book is a searching study of all forms of sham, deceit, and hypocrisy. A triumph in mobility, the story has no unity of action, or ascension to a climax. The curtain is dropped as abruptly as it is raised, and the last chapter, far from gathering up the scattered strands, reveals more loose ends, and the reader stumbles at this late hour upon the unexplored world of young schoolboys, about whose lives, if these are to be judged by their vitiated beginnings, only the first word has been spoken. "I should like to terminate my novel," he explains, "with the words 'it could continue indefinitely,' for I consider that life offers nothing which might not be looked upon as a fresh starting point as well as a conclusion."

If Gide and most of his heroes are to be pronounced moral, they must base their claims on a very special code of ethics. They must jeer at all traditions and social hypocrisies; indeed, at any semblance of a root or tie. Ménalque, the Mephistophelian hero of *Les Nourritures terrestres,* is Gide's mouthpiece when he says: "Family, I hate you! Sheltered homes, closed doors, jealous custodians of happiness!" This aversion includes any spot that brings repose, consistent affection, or attachment to ideas. Hence, perhaps, Gide's passion for travel, which he urges upon everyone, and his championship of every vagabond and restless spirit like himself, whether he be Baudelaire or the Prodigal Son. For him the most interesting and worthwhile personality is always the tormented one. His preference is for the outcast, and his sympathy is invariably engaged by the adventurer, the illegitimate child, the unwholesome or delinquent character. This tendency is revealed in his secret connivance with all law breakers and marauders, particularly if these happen to be boys. "The worst instincts," says his *Immoraliste,* "have always seemed to me the most sincere." Or again, speaking in his own name: "I earnestly hope to experience every passion, every vice—at least, I have always sponsored them." It is because of Gide's curiosity in regard to the unorthodox, his countenance of all subversive tendencies, that many felt justified in denouncing him as a dangerous, corrupting influence.

However, if Gide advocates nonconformity and the 'dangerous' life, he contends that this independence must first be justified through a critical examination of one's soul. With his own soul he experimented all his life, and his work, always interrogatory in spirit, resembles one long debate. He not only stands in perpetual curiosity before himself and the world at large, but his principal characters are invested with this same inquisitive introspection. Most of them keep private journals, which either constitute the entire story, or play an important part in the development of the plot. When these heroes and heroines do not possess a diary of their own, they are apt to be seen, as Pierre-Quint in his study of Gide points out, forcing drawers, opening sealed letters, or stealing valises, to discover other peoples' secrets.

Always amenable to persuasion, never thoroughly convinced by his own arguments, Gide is constantly alert for conflicting testimony. Prometheus is represented in the end as eating his eagle and feeling all the better for it. *La Porte étroite* is at once a satire and a eulogy of asceticism. Ménalque, after preaching throughout some two hundred pages of *Les Nourritures terrestres,* says: "Throw away my book, and know that my attitude in face of life is only one of a thousand others." It is characteristic that on one page of his notebook Gide would inscribe an opinion only to expose its fallacy on the opposite page. "I am a creature of dialogue," he writes, "and everything in me fights and contradicts itself." Born of a Norman, Catholic mother, and a Protestant father from Languedoc, he reminds us frequently of this dual strain in his blood. Nothing is more indicative of his nature than the books he loved most as a child. These were the Bible and *The Thousand and One Nights,* which he read with equal fervor. "People either love or fail to understand the Bible," he explains in *Prétextes,* "love or fail to understand *The Thousand and One Nights.* But I, if you please, divide the world of thinkers into two classes, and that because of their irreconcilable types of intelligence: those who are moved in the face of these two books, and those for whom they have no meaning." In order to define his position, he transforms the axiom of *les extrêmes se touchent* into *les extrêmes me touchent,* and says: "I have always been attracted by those opinions which are elusive, and by extreme divergencies of thought. Each spirit interests me only in that which makes it differ from the others." Again speaking through Ménalque, he says: "I have made myself flexible, kindly disposed and free for all my senses. I have become such an attentive listener that I no longer maintain a single personal thought, capturing every emotion in its passage, and reacting so slightly to everything that I consider nothing evil." At first sight, Gide's intelligence seems unusually sane and balanced; with greater familiarity, we perceive a touch of disease in a mind incapable of option.

Of his religion, he writes: "I am neither a Protestant nor a Catholic; I am a Christian." At times he calls himself a believer in the very letter of the Gospels; at others, a heretic among heretics. As he deems religion a very personal affair and prefers that everything which passes between Jehovah and himself should remain secret, it is difficult to determine just what Gide means by God. Certainly the mystic fervor of his early years was profoundly modified by time, and dating from *Les Nourri-tures terrestres,* sensation and artistic sensuality constitute his credo. But to define him as a sensualist means to forget those other moments of deep religious feeling. Perhaps no other modern writer resorts more frequently to scriptural citation. Whatever his metamorphosis, one feels the conscientious moral struggle which preceded it. Rejecting every ready-made formula, Gide thought out each problem for himself, and built up his life on the solid rock of sincerity. His goal was to attain the innocence of the little child, "the infant who is naked but feels no shame therefrom," and revealing his poignant quest for moral peace, he cries: "When shall I be able, far from morose thoughts, to divulge my complete joy bathed by the sunlight; and in complete forgetfulness of yesterday and of so many religions, embrace the happiness which will come in perfect abundance, without scruples, without fear?"

Prior to the War, Gide was not regarded as a very serious influence, nor were his early books a great success. *Les Cahiers d'André Walter,* published at first anonymously, had few readers, and Gide hesitated several years before consenting to republish it. He showed no ambition for a brilliant literary career. Taunted by a cousin who said: "You will never make me believe that you will not stick to the first literary *genre* in which you will be successful," Gide replied: "But I prefer not to succeed than be limited to any single style of composition. Even were it to lead to the highest honors, I could not consent to follow an indicated path. I prefer the adventurous, the hazardous, the unknown, and to be where I am least expected. Above all, I wish to be left in peace and able to think freely." Although Gide occupied a conspicuous position in the literary world as founder of the revolutionary *Nouvelle Revue Française,* which first appeared in 1909, it was not until after the World War, more precisely around the year 1920, that he came into his own and was hailed as a leader of the younger generation. *Corydon* and *Si le grain ne meurt* attracted wide attention, indeed created scandal, and after the phenomenal success of *Les Faux-Monnayeurs* Gide was the most widely discussed writer of his day, with editors making haste to reprint his earlier works.

More even than for the intrinsic literary value of his work, he will be remembered for the direction he gave to a whole generation of uneasy, groping minds. "My rôle is to disturb," he announced, and in an age of skeptical disillusionment when everyone, as one critic expressed it, was on vacation and wondering when classes would be resumed, Gide led the way to the only school whose rules would be obeyed, the school of playing truant. As a man who proclaimed: "My heart beats only in sympathy, it is for others that I exist, as though by proxy or espousal, and I can only live intensely when I escape from myself to become no matter who"; as one who, like his own hero in *Les Nourritures terrestres,* was writing "so that later some adolescent such as I was at sixteen, but one less bound, more daring and accomplished, may find in my book a response to his own palpitating interrogation"; Gide delighted in furnishing disquieting and contradictory arguments and in rendering the young intelligence critically self-aware. Over many a rebellious spirit his doctrines exerted a disintegrating influence; in arousing others from their moral lethargy, his teachings proved salutary. Of late years he has written little, and has devoted himself to social problems. Urged by his sense of equity and sympathy for suffering, he championed the cause of the Nigerian negroes against the cruelty and stupidity of their governors. He recently created a sensation by pronouncing himself a communist, a step which he says he has been considering for some forty years. "What has brought me to communism," he writes in his recently published *Pages de journal,* "is not Marx, but the Gospels. It is they which have inculcated in me doubt as to my own value, and respect for the thought and value of others. They have fortified in me that disdain and repugnance, doubtless inherent in me, for all private possession and monopoly." Gide's latest attitude is that of the

Monsieur who scorns all benefit arising from intellectual privilege.

However debatable may be his views, Gide's skill in transcribing them is flawless. Fluid, rhythmic, supple, his language rivals in purity the great masters of French Classicism. Indeed, they were his models, for wishing to remain classic in form, he avoids the word bigger than the thought. In spite of a rich and resourceful vocabulary, he is sparing in his use of words. Rarely resorting to imagery, he considers all unnecessary ornament an impediment to thought. Gide's style needs no embellishment; his natural lucidity of mind finds its most spontaneous expression in simple, transparent prose. The literary form he most admires and has himself achieved is a fulness of breath and life, transmuted into art through the enameled beauty of words.

Jean Giraudoux [1]

GIRAUDOUX provokes superlatives only. Some readers find him unique among all the contemporary French novelists; to others he is the greatest bore. Lucien Dubech calls him the worst writer of his generation; Boulenger esteems him the most original: "Nothing that Giraudoux says, not the slightest little thing, has been said before." Evidently the Giraudoux variety of humor appeals to certain fortunate temperaments alone. His admirers do not even resent the Encyclopaedia, the Larousse, the atlas, the mythological manual, the herbal, and the numerous technical dictionaries to which they find themselves condemned. The cryptic allusions strewn along his path may refer to some minor political figure, to an obscure Persian legend, or a "dalaganpalang," but Giraudoux has no intention of providing further elucidation. He prepares delightful knots which you must untie for yourself. These literary feasts are offered by an exacting Amphitryon, and many a passage requires a second reading, but in spite of stumblingblocks, you never measure with impatient fingers the diminishing pages.

Though he is frequently imitated, and though he is only one among many exponents of a similar literary creed, he has always been acclaimed the unrivaled master of his genre—if such a prodigal assortment as *L'Ecole des indifférents, Siegfried et le Limousin, Suzanne et le Pacifique, Juliette au pays des hommes, Simon le pathétique, Adorable Clio, Elpénor, Bella,*

[1] This essay was published in *The Bookman*, March 1933.

Eglantine, Jérôme Bardini, and *Combat avec l'ange,* can be said to belong to any school but his own. Indeed the hours of entertainment Giraudoux provides are outside of all schools or creeds. Nor does the term 'entertainment' imply a light regard for his art. Giraudoux makes us laugh, and that is a serious accomplishment. If he demands his reader's coöperation and makes him work for his diversion, the rare quality of this diversion justifies the arduous literary form.

After all, it is only the thorny coating, not the thought beneath, which proves so disconcerting. Under this formidable, if brilliant, exterior, the most genial of virtuosi reveals himself. Giraudoux is a scholar, but if he exploits his learning, it is only for the embellishment of his wit. In spite of the snake-charmers, the poets, the exiled Russians, the Interior Monologues, figuring in Juliette's expedition to the "land of men" (*Juliette au pays des hommes*), this young woman is at heart a simple and guileless soul, taking one last, chaste fling before returning to the handsome young fiancé awaiting her in the provinces. And what curious knowledge she brings to this reunion as a result of her various adventures! "How little you know, Gérard! You are ignorant of the fact that the Assyrio-Chaldæans did not believe in original sin. Ignorant of the date of the crowning of Sapor, perhaps even of his fall. Not aware that in the city of Saintes it is a dog that rings the Angelus." The acquisition of these important facts, however, does not prevent the young lovers from bickering over a new dressing gown or from throwing themselves into each other's arms. If Suzanne, after her six long years of exile on an abandoned Polynesian island (*Suzanne et le Pacifique*), has new visions of life, they assume no more disquieting proportions than her eagerness to return to cows and men, where she may have living "milk-trees," human "hug-trees," and perhaps an omelette.

It does not take long to discover that Giraudoux is having

a thoroughly good time, not only amusing himself, but gloating, like a precocious child, at the picture of a mystified audience. The audacity and unexpectedness of his imagery is obviously intended to cause a gasp; and gasp you do until the rapid-fire succession of acrobatics defeats its own end and leaves you stunned.

He is the least spontaneous of writers. Designedly artificial and *précieux,* his most irresistible witticisms are at the same time the most studied. It is on this very artificiality that he counts largely for his comic effects. By means of it he produces such passages as: "It was the week when the acacias perfumed the air, and we ate them in fritters; when the larks dotted the skies, and we ate them in tarts; when the rye became all golden and had its single day of triumph over the wheat, and we had pancakes." It is safe to assert that there is not a single banal line in his fifteen or more books, and this is largely due to the application of just such carefully calculated artifices. To avoid being commonplace he will resort to any trick. Fortunately his ingenuity is inexhaustible. Giraudoux's sun never does anything so prosaic as "set"; it lingers for a moment behind the hills "like an actor ready to return at applause." When Suzanne's eyebrows are described, we learn that "when it rained, they kept the water from trickling down her face; and, since they met, her nose was also sheltered!"

Perhaps Giraudoux was one of those whom Gide had in mind when he wrote: "How fatiguing is that mania of certain literary men who cannot see one object without immediately thinking of another." Certainly Giraudoux is possessed of what Gide calls the "demon of analogy." Who else would compare small fish escaping from the rear of a cart to "tears in the dust," "commas in mourning"? What will he say, never said before, about a cloud? That it is "painted and powdered like Esther before her king." To be sure, one suspects at times that this imagery is rather the result of a system than of an inspiration. Yet even when far-fetched, his analogies are welcome additions if only for their fantastic association of ideas and their sheer nonsense. That is why we are glad that Suzanne felt gaiety "hung from her face by a thousand clips, like a piece of linen about to flutter," and why, upon encountering the Ugliest-in-the-World-Bird, she discovered in it "all the minor maladies so humiliating to tenors and young husbands: boils, corns, a sty, and a sneeze."

Equally arbitrary is his use of violent antithesis, usually recognizable as mere toying with effect rather than contributing to the thought content. Juliette has one warm hand so that the other may be cold. Giraudoux's young doctors have aged patients only, his old doctors have youthful ones; his song-birds perch above the mute-birds; his night-birds collide with his day-birds. We are not surprised, therefore, when in *Siegfried et le Limousin,* Geneviève thus describes the alternation of her lovers: "A man of mature years, a youth, a man of mature years, a youth, never a man of my own age. Every eighteen months I was certain to capture a white beard, to fall back again at the end of the eighteen months on extreme youth and help my friend prepare his college examinations."

Some critics find in Giraudoux a man of abnormally acute sensibilities, who perceives through strangely colored spectacles a universe which the ordinary mortal must gaze upon with less enlightened eyes. It would be nearer the truth to say that he is an extraordinarily clever man who has consciously adopted these spectacles. If he did not possess ordinary vision, how explain his invariable ability to depart from it? Is not a part of his strategy revealed by Suzanne's confession: "I see as you do not know how to see, for I have not yet regained the habit of separating the physical from the moral"? So she endows trees, birds, streams, and all forms of nature with thought and human attributes. When she thinks of a man it is of his "two large moustaches and a limitless devotion"; of his "palpitating Adam's apple and a great need of confidence"; of his "sheathed scarf-pin and a sweet obstinacy." This willful interweaving of the sublime with the ridiculous is eminently characteristic and constitutes one of his greatest, if studiously cultivated, charms.

His usual procedure consists first in the simple statement of a thought, then its development by humorously realistic illustration. The more commonplace the thought the more original the illustration, for with Giraudoux it is the concrete example, not the abstract idea, on which his fancy plays variations. He tells us (in *Juliette au pays des hommes*) that Juliette was careful, and then he adds: "She was the girl who had lost the fewest handkerchiefs in her life." Her fiancé, Gérard, is introduced in the opening scene as a lazy, healthy young animal lying in the sun. Giraudoux wishes to show that his hero's physical well-being is of more real moment than all the social and material advantages acquired through the efforts of his ancestors. To drive home his point, he balances these two ideas against each other, and piles up his comic effect. (1) Gérard is sucking at a straw, and—equivalent blessing—he possesses an income of 200,000 francs. (2) A blackbird casts its shadow on his face, and—equal pressure on his soul—the silhouette of a rich, pure fiancée named Juliette. (3) The voluptuous itching of an eczema has attacked his foot, and—he is a descendant of Guizot. (4) He amuses himself by playing with a thistle, and—he owns a Hispano-Suiza.

This presentation of the general in terms of the specific, the significant in terms of the insignificant, leads him into all forms of exaggeration, obviously and gratuitously absurd. For example, Suzanne claims that striped antelopes should inspire a love for wise men and poets. Giraudoux's abuse of the superlative "the only," "the last," "the most," frequently makes him a rival of one of his own characters, the actress who with false ingenuousness applies the qualifying term of "first" to all her experiences, even to a certain banquet, the first occasion of her eating rice. Giraudoux is inclined to sum up whole nations by some ludicrously concrete image. Germany suffers the most in this respect. This is the nation, he informs us, which "to pass its life and time, has invented beer, war, the Jew's harp, and a large number of irregular verbs." It is the country where "taxi-cab fares mount by 22½, and horses find more shade in April at the foot of obelisks and mausoleums than under trees."

No character escapes his ridicule, not even his beautiful young heroines, sometimes the most clownish of them all. His nonsense may appear at the most unexpected moments. It may descend on Marie Belliard, who being a drug addict, "turns her little nose curiously towards the Duke of Sarignon; he did not merit so much honor, having merely washed his fountain pen in ether." Or upon the archæologist who, upon seeing Juliette's eyes, one of which was blue, the other brown, was reminded of the cats of Erzerum, which have one blue eye and one gray; this made the good man instinctively raise his voice, since these cats are deaf. Or upon American men "who come to France to study the architecture of happiness in the hearts of French women, thereafter departing at a gallop for Minneapolis to implant it in the hearts of gigantic young girls usually named Watson." It is worth struggling through all the obscurities of *Elpénor* to be rewarded from time to time with such preposterous bits as the picture of the Cyclops weeping as he milks his ewes, "his tears falling into the cream, which curdled, so that on that day he made the most delicious of his cheeses." Or his buffoonery may pursue every movement of a character, as in the case of Suzanne's governess, "all of whose possessions were shaky and fragile—two or three teeth, and a pin which closed badly. She returned every evening with a purchase and some part repaired: a hat of red duvetine when her eyetooth was filed; a fan when her toenail was straightened."

Sometimes it is a whole chapter of grotesque fun, such as the account of Juliette's scuffle in the property room of the Opéra (*Juliette au pays des hommes*), where she seeks to avoid the kiss of the innocuous opera singer Boris. Here Giraudoux provides a laugh for every line, from the moment when Juliette feels all synthetic matter on her person disintegrating before the attack: her false pearls, her shoelaces of false leather, her hatpin of false steel, her right earring, which was of paste. The destruction of each object convinces her that women should adorn themselves in diamonds and platinum only, and be wary of adulterated wool and artificial silk. She frantically turns on gas jets and water spigots, flings cosmetics, snatches at wooden swords and pistols, her screams unheeded because mistaken for those of a rehearsing Rhine maiden. She finally escapes from her exhausted admirer's arms by scratching him, and the sight of blood attracts a solicitous band of ballet dancers from the wings. Mindful of infection and the dangerous monthly presence of the Valkyrie horse, these young women recommend an anti-tetanus injection, while Juliette blandly accepts Boris' dinner invitation for that evening.

This humor lapses at times into horseplay, but even Giraudoux's slapstick has quality. Juliette becomes a sort of Simple Simon in her quest for celebrated men, and Suzanne rivals Charlie Chaplin as she strikes at one wasp and accidently kills another. All this is very diverting, but creates at times a false atmosphere, especially in scenes involving his heroines, though usually these are only the author in feminine disguise.

Frequently Giraudoux utilizes his wit as a *sauce piquante* to serve up his inner irony. He is caustic but never bitter, in spite of certain pet aversions. The Comédie Française is one of these, with its "old Jewish actress speaking with an English accent and named Céorelle." Rarely does he praise foreign countries, though he is prodigal in exposing their oddities—or what he chooses to select as such. The shipwrecked Suzanne (*Suzanne et le Pacifique*), comfortably nude on her deserted island, speculates as to how men of different nationalities would greet her: the polished Englishman, extending his hand, would say: "Excuse my glove"; the American pastor, draping her in his university pennant, would quickly make a photograph; while the German, installing her at a folding table, in front of Pilsener beer, would condemn her to a kiss every time she forgot to shut the pewter cover of her stein. Giraudoux asserts that when Americans were considered English, they fought against the English; when they became American, they had a civil war; and when sufficiently German in their culture, they flew to arms against the Germans—the first American to take a prisoner in 1917 being named Meyer, as was the man he captured.

Although a far traveler, Giraudoux is anything but international in spirit. Remaining resolutely French, he perceptibly softens his satire when his native country is in question. Accordingly, when the French woman, Geneviève, and the German Eva, both courtesans and of approximately the same walk in life, are placed side by side, the French woman is represented as seeking the corner "which will most seclude her like a pearl," the German choosing the spot "where the municipality would have erected a fountain or a statue." Giraudoux is as violent a nationalist as he dare be without jeopardizing his reputation as a clever and amusing man. In *Siegfried et le Limousin,* the repatriation of the French soldier Forestier, suffering from amnesia and believing himself a German, provides him with material for an effective satire of post-war Germany. Through their eagerness to utilize this Frenchman's logical and intuitive mind in their affairs of state, the Germans admit the lack of just those qualities in their own mentality. France he desires to show as the "world's comptroller of Weights and Measures"; everything is superior there; its air is purer, its sky is bluer. In *Suzanne et le Pacifique,* he pictures the harmony that a French mind, and a French mind only, can bestow upon the wilds of nature. The German way of meeting life on an uninhabited island is illustrated by Robinson Crusoe, who came from Bremen, as contrasted with the French, represented by Suzanne, who is from Limousin. Crusoe, as Giraudoux reminds us, littered his island with household conveniences such as porringers and stew-pans, just as his nation was later to encumber the world with shop-made goods and tin plate; the French girl, on the contrary, leisurely enjoys the facilities which nature has already provided. "You," says Suzanne to the imaginary Robinson, "you speak of the flavor of birds and never of their song. Don't work for three months to make a table: squat. Don't lose six months in making a *prie-Dieu:* kneel down where you are." The fact that *Robinson Crusoe* was the work of an Englishman is of small importance, for Giraudoux has made his point. Perhaps he agrees with Oscar Wilde, who lauds those literary masterpieces where "facts are either kept in their proper subordinate position, or else entirely excluded on the general ground of dullness."

As for the World War, Giraudoux chooses to avoid the broader issues of the conflict and confine himself to his own very special reactions. Throughout *Adorable Clio,* where he relates his war experiences, he reveals himself as a man who, though not lacking in sensibility, deliberately suppresses it in order to concentrate on the more subtle phases of the conflict. After introducing his readers to the various battle-fronts, what does he show them as a result of so much sacrifice and suffering? Himself seated at a café table after the Armistice, where, by squinting his eyes, he sees everything with a golden contour. It is Sunday and the noon of a beautiful day. For most people this would be a glorious feeling, but all that Giraudoux portrays is a man who has become thoroughly benumbed, a Stoic and not a very happy one.

Most of Giraudoux's books are riotous medleys of wit and satire rather than novels in the ordinary sense. The stories are at best fragmentary; the plots, episodic and very thinly sketched; nothing is farther from his thoughts than the creation of living people. Presented through their foibles only, from some amusing or eccentric angle, his characters amount to hardly more than droll phantoms, mannikins on which to drape his wit. It may be Emmanuel Ratier, who is so vain that he ceases to admire famous men the moment he himself has passed the age of their greatest exploits; or Juliette Lartigue, whose eyes shine when she is hungry, whose mouth waters at the purchase of perfumes, whose nose quivers at the mention of God. All that we know of Victoria is that she has a 17 ankle and a 30 calf. In this entire gallery you will search in vain for a credible person—or, it must be added, a dull one.

To follow a character through a graduated psychological development would only bore him. Impatient and whimsical, he presents people ready made, with a spotlight thrown now here, now there, on the feature he desires to emphasize. In *Juliette au pays des hommes* he has carried out a more consecutive experiment. Already in her twenties when, abandoning temporarily her fiancé, she goes to Paris in search of potential husbands and knowledge of the world, Juliette is emotionally still an adolescent. Just as to a baby a grown person seems a giant, to Juliette, still thinking as a schoolgirl, Boris the tenor seems to symbolize her most romantic dreams. Thus, her contact with reality is rendered all the more absurd. In *Suzanne et le Pacifique* this idea is presented in reverse. Here a sophisticated young woman suddenly finds herself confronted with the primitive. These tropical glades remind her of dressmaking establishments; the auroral lights suggest trolley-car signals; the birds represent aigrettes and ostrich plumes for hats; the flowers mean so many varieties of perfumery. The rich young Maléna in *Combat avec l'ange* belongs to the species known as happy people, a child-woman whose organs for contemplating the misery of the world have become atrophied through lack of use. Hence disgust, pity, vanity, and jealousy are unknown to her and she sets out in quest of all of them. Still another search is Jérôme Bardini's flight to America, where in the spontaneous irresponsibility of an incognito existence he hopes to escape from the banal monotony of life and regain his social and moral liberty.

Giraudoux is chiefly interested in his heroines. He probably would be better pleased if he could write novels without the intrusion of a single male. Does he not isolate Suzanne on an uninhabited island throughout the major portion of his book? Fashioned from a single mold, all of his young women are radiant and beautiful without physical or moral blemish; sensible and resolute, they may emerge for a moment into the troubled maelstrom of life but are always led safely home to the calm waters of reason and the simple life. Although they indulge in inner monologues, and Suzanne, for one, has ample leisure for reflection, we learn little if anything of their minds. Young men are either omitted altogether from his novels or assigned subordinate rôles. His heroines seem perfectly satisfied with the middle-aged men provided for them, for Giraudoux makes them rich and socially prominent. They either possess titles, occupy important official posts, or are wealthy financiers. In addition, they are gentle, gallant, discreet, placid, and suitably jealous.

Since the world is neither sufficiently absurd nor beautiful to suit Giraudoux, he turns it inside out and redecorates it. "I wish to live," he writes, "in blissful oblivion of reality, with all its contours modified and velvet-soft so that my eyes will not be wounded." No social or ethical discussion mars the glistening serenity of his pages. He is not interested in reforming the world, only in forgetting it. He is happiest when his subject matter adapts itself readily to the bizarre and fanciful, although he finds few situations too commonplace to be transformed by some odd twist into the strange and unaccountable. *Suzanne et le Pacifique* is one of the most successful of his works, for in this book he creates a *Wonderland*. The exotic island where Suzanne is wrecked is an ideal hunting ground for his adventurous fancy; and in such a background this French Alice can indulge her author in his most unbridled vagaries. She can adorn her nakedness with red feathers—in the midst of a thousand gorgeous birds—all the flora and fauna of which Giraudoux has ever heard. She can have two blue parrots when she eats bananas, two diving-birds when she opens oysters, two orange wagtails when she gathers mangoes—a distribution typical of Giraudoux. Here the flowers taste like young pig or resemble soaps, and the caverns shine as though with electric bulbs from the reflection of the red birds entangled in them. Naturally the first fruit picked by Suzanne is exactly ripe, making her feel that "for thousands of years the race between her destiny and this mango has been timed to the second."

So nothing surprises in Giraudoux—or rather, everything does. Every extravaganza may be found, but never—and here he occupies a unique position among his contemporaries—the vulgar or obscene. The most modest young girl need have no fear of him. He not only adores young girls but is said to be eager to include them in his public. A few of his heroines, like Bella, have pasts, but Giraudoux's treatment is sufficiently delicate to satisfy the most punctilious. Of course, this is only mock decorum on his part—witness his clever and sophisticated use of innuendo—but it is decorum nevertheless.

His charm escapes dissection. I have permitted myself so many quotations because his flavor is better tasted than described. He errs in being too generous. Mannerisms and tricks of style, repeated too often, have a banality of their own, and Giraudoux does not escape the monotony which results from perpetual imitation of himself. His abuse of imagery becomes as devitalizing as the adjectives and adverbs this imagery is intended to supplant. He can be best enjoyed in instalments, in chapters picked at random.

Of recent years—beginning with *Les Aventures de Jérôme Bardini* (1930) and including *Combat avec l'ange* (1934)— Giraudoux has cast a more thoughtful glance around him, and become conscious of the real world engulfed in uneasiness and doubt. Identifying himself at last with other writers of his generation, he has consented to envisage social problems. In changing his mood, he changes his manner and writes in more somber vein. The habitual smile is there, but is now tinged with the slightest shade of weariness. There is less spontaneous gaiety, and he no longer seems inclined to dazzle and surprise. Can it be that he, like Juliette, has had his fling, and has renounced his early frivolity, alas! for the more serious, humdrum thinking of advancing years?

François Mauriac

MAURIAC's election to the French Academy rekindled interest in this distinguished writer. His sensitive, almost tragic features were photographed for every French newspaper and illustrated review. It is a sad face which suggests some inner torment. Harassed by the lifelong struggle between his religious and literary integrity, this good Catholic and brilliant novelist appears never to have enjoyed an easy moment. Not since Racine—whose problems were in some respects identical—has a writer professed such qualms of conscience. But fortunately for us, Mauriac has not yet followed the example of his illustrious predecessor and ceased to write. The world—the Roman Catholic world, at least—is still eagerly awaiting his final stand. In the meanwhile, Mauriac suffers—and we have good novels.

To the layman, the polemics waged in Mauriac's name resemble a tempest in a teapot. Neither Mauriac himself, nor the people he portrays, seem so very reprehensible. Indeed, these characters are almost virtuous when compared with the creations of many of his contemporaries. It may appear incredible that a twentieth-century novelist should concern himself so seriously with winning the good graces of the Church. By this, I do not mean that the modern man has ceased to scrutinize his soul; in truth, most of our writers do little else. They are all seeking salvation in some form or other, and many, like Mauriac, preach a return to God. But there are few who identify themselves so closely with religious dogma. Mauriac has done every-

thing in the world to win the approbation of the Church—
everything, that is, except comply servilely with her demands.

Born in the shadow of the cathedral at Bordeaux, bereaved
of his father when an infant, Mauriac was brought up under
his mother's guidance in the strictest orthodoxy. In one of his
autobiographical accounts, he relates how every morning at
nine the family group would assemble in his mother's room
and kneel in prayer. "At what age was I first touched by our
admirable diocesan prayer? It seems to me that from my very
infancy this incantation moved me." However, religion, as
Mauriac's family conceived it, was a compound of pettiness
and grandeur. It was the source of his early joys and consolations, as it was the cause of his youthful terrors and scruples.
Looking back upon this period of his life, he asks himself:
"Why, then, was I such an unhappy lad?"

The mysteries of religion found a sympathetic soil in a nature
sensitive, solitary, and physically weak. He tells us he was a
sickly child, that he was not a good student, that he disliked
the games and sports of his playmates, and that he felt no
love for anyone but his mother. Melancholy in the thought
that no one loved him, he took refuge in tears and resignation.
"I was born with a full knowledge of this desert—life—and was
resigned in advance never to emerge from it." Although in any
environment Mauriac would probably have remained the impressionable, mystic youth, the dreaming poet and the esthete
of his early years, it was at his country home in the neighborhood of Bordeaux that he first discovered that love of nature
would provide an outlet for emotion. Here he immersed himself in the wind, the pines, the vineyards, the intense heat of
the noonday sun, and longed for some companion. He had an
ardent nature, and if he was fervent in his religious beliefs, he
was likewise assailed by the temptations of awakening adolescence. Like Claude, the youthful hero of *La Chair et le sang,*

he soon found his idealistic temperament maladjusted to the realities of life, and his healthy body incapable of submitting to a purely spiritual existence. This conflict was to become the great problem of his life, as it became the theme of many of his novels; in a word, the inspiration and the torment of his artistic career. Far from resolving his difficulties as time went on, Mauriac never outgrew his prolonged adolescence; he never ceased to experience the guilty delectation of the child who gazes upon forbidden fruit. Whether or not he had a taste for sin, he stood ever fascinated before the forbidden mysteries of the senses.

Although best known as a novelist, Mauriac has written numerous essays either on his own life or that of kindred spirits. The titles of a few of these reveal their nature: *Petits essais de psychologie religieuse; Le jeune homme; La rencontre avec Pascal; Le tourment de Jacques Rivière; La vie de Racine; Supplément au traité de la concupiscence; Mes plus lointains souvenirs; Trois grands hommes devant Dieu; Souffrance et bonheur du Chrétien; Commencements d'une vie; Le romancier et ses personnages.* In addition to this self-revealing material, there is one especially significant document, *Dieu et Mammon,* in which Mauriac recounts the genesis of his spiritual life and describes the ordeal of the devout Catholic who is at the same time a creative artist.

He avers that Catholicism was the cause of his unhappiness. It was a religion imposed at birth, and for an impressionable nature such as Mauriac's, this was tantamount to the exclusion of all further choice. The more he strove to cast off his religious bonds, the more tenaciously they clung, and his faith survived, as it were, in spite of him. Confronted by two masters, the spirit and the flesh, he found the flesh slowly but surely gaining the upper hand: hence his despair of ever attaining an equilibrium between God and Mammon.

His literary beginnings were made under Roman Catholic auspices, and from the first he complains of the Church's disapproval. It demanded that he be a proselytizer. As an artist he claimed the privilege of detachment. How reconcile the artistic instinct with the writing of books intended primarily to edify? Convinced that the clergy were exhibiting a form of stupidity peculiar to the Catholic mind, he continued to write in his own fashion.

However, this decision brought him little peace, for he suspected that his critics were not altogether wrong in detecting a decadent element in his works. He sought every opportunity to vindicate himself; in numerous pamphlets he defined—and he hoped, justified—his relation and responsibility towards his public and his Church. He would not admit that Catholicism itself was unsound, but he pronounced it impracticable because of the shortsighted interpretation of the priests. Was he not discharging some part of his religious responsibility, he asks, by attracting the world's attention to existing discrepancies in Catholic teachings?

As a Christian writer, he was obliged to choose between his own convictions and the creation of characters whose views he did not share. In either case, if these views were found to be unorthodox, the Catholics would condemn him. Mauriac contends that the Catholic novelist is no more privileged than any other to falsify the life he sees around him, and he asks why those who profess to believe in the original fall and corruption of humanity are unwilling to look either squarely in the face? "Impossible to reproduce the modern world," he writes, "without portraying the violation of some holy law," and he laments the necessity of altering his creation through fear of wounding the susceptibilities of impressionable readers. What, for instance, is his own responsibility towards the young man who, as a result of reading *Génitrix,* sent him his photograph with the inscription: "To the man who almost made me kill my grand-mother!"

It is interesting to recall that Gide—though the last to worry about responsibilities—expresses much the same idea when he says: "How many secret Werthers were ignorant of themselves, were only awaiting the reading of Goethe's novel, to commit suicide! How many hidden heroes needed only the example of a book, some spark escaped from this fictitious life, before following the lead!"

Mauriac is well aware of the truth of Gide's statements that "exalted feelings are the stuff of which bad literature is made"; that "there is no work of art to which the Demon is not a co-signatory"; and that "there are no artists amongst the saints, no saints amongst the artists." He knew also that souls in a state of pristine purity do not exist; that they are to be found only in fiction, and bad fiction at that. In order to obey the strict letter of religious law, the Christian would have to abandon all idea of writing novels, and Mauriac wonders if the genuine novelist could ever make so great a sacrifice. He believes that the real artist is no more master of his creative imagination than he is of his own destiny. "The moment a character conforms docilely to what is expected of him, the author may rest assured that no life remains in his inanimate puppet." (*Le Romancier et ses personnages.*)

To follow the development of Mauriac's art is to follow the various stages of his moral growth, for his life and his art are inextricably interwoven. The novels which reflect his spiritual evolution gain in depth and strength as Mauriac climbs arduously the rungs of his own moral ladder. He was to find no lasting protection or solace in his faith until he accomplished his own conversion. Nor was he persuaded at a single stroke and for all time; it was a long, ever renewed fight, demanding the greatest fortitude and perseverance.

Defining the art of writing novels as "a transposition of the real and not a reproduction of the real," he believes that a novelist must pass his characters through the sieve of his personal experience and then conceive them as living individuals who work out their own destinies. "There comes that moment in every novelist's life," he writes, "when, after having struggled for years to create what he believes to be new types, he ends by discovering that it has only been the same character reappearing in one novel after another. Indeed, the books which a novelist has already composed are only the earlier drafts of a work which he has been striving to realize without success. His problem is not to multiply his types, but with infinite patience to renew the same character in the hope that some day he will produce that masterpiece which he has been pursuing from the beginning, but which, perhaps, he will never be able to write." This character, of course, is Mauriac himself. He has transported his own inner conflict into each new book, and it is this recurrent theme which gives, in spite of the variety of its wrappings, a fundamental unity to his work. "When my critics demand that I try something new, I say to myself that the essential thing is to go to new depths in my original subject. If people complain that the hero of *Le Nœud de vipères* resembles too greatly that of *Génitrix,* this criticism does not disturb me, because in this later work I am assured of having penetrated deeper into the knowledge of this man, of having brought to light a more hidden layer of his being." In these potential Mauriacs the author seeks some solution, or at least some compromise for his own difficulties. His books are so many conquests over his own timidities and uncertainties; in short, so many scenes in his own moral drama. Hence, he says: "For a long time, I believed that an author's work delivered him from all that lay dormant in him, such as desires, angers, spites; that his erring characters were the scapegoats for all his own potential sins; that, on the other hand, the superman, the demigod, accomplished the heroic acts of which he was incapable; thus, he transferred to them his own good or evil impulses."

Mauriac's novels fall into three rather sharply defined divisions. The first group comprises *L'Enfant chargé de chaînes, La Robe prétexte,* written just before the War, and *La Chair et le sang,* which appeared soon after it. His first novels, portraying very youthful souls, reveal the author's hesitations as a Catholic in face of religious doubts, worldly ambitions, and his craving for a frankly voluptuous life. In conformity with Catholic teaching, he was expected to represent all earthly love as antagonistic to the love of God. As a young man, Mauriac strove to reconcile the two, but found the experiment disastrous. "It is difficult," writes Lucien Dubech in commenting on Mauriac's early work, "to love or take very seriously these young Catholics, who, scarcely issuing from the church, lose all their illusions at Montmartre, where they go to dissipate between vespers and morning prayer. Returning home with pasty mouths at early dawn, they shed a tear over the fate of the workmen and maidservants they see hastening to their daily labor."

After his next novel, *Préséances,* which marks a period of transition, Mauriac emerges from the troubled, adolescent groping characteristic of his early work, and with *Le Baiser au lépreux* (1922) begins a series of infinitely more mature and skilful novels: *Le Fleuve de feu; Génitrix; Le désert de l'amour; Coups de couteaux; Thérèse Desqueyroux;* and *Destins* (1928). In this second period of his career, Mauriac may be called a Catholic and a novelist, but not a Catholic novelist. If, as Charles du Bos points out in *François Mauriac et le problème du romancier catholique,* Mauriac the novelist gains much from Mauriac the Catholic, the contrary is not true. The Catholic in Mauriac reaps nothing from this association, unless it be the hatred which was to burst forth one day in *Destins.*

Mauriac limited his field of observation almost exclusively to Bordeaux and its countryside. No one was better equipped to scourge the numerous defects found in certain old provincial Catholic families. Who but an eye-witness could evoke so faithfully this world of petty vanities and dissension, of demoralizing avarice, jealousy, spite, hatred, pride, and snobbery? His *dramatis personae* may be divided into those central figures whose psychology is the special object of his study, and the minor characters who serve as buffers or motivators. Among these lesser figures are representatives from all classes of Bordeaux society. Treated with bitter scorn because of their bestiality and lack of true spirituality, they create a somber and depressing atmosphere through which his main figures struggle and meet defeat. His satire is directed most keenly at members of the Catholic faith whose religion consists of a strict adherence to prescribed forms. In *Le Nœud de vipères,* Janine, the granddaughter of the old man who is writing the story, has been abandoned by her husband; to the question "Do you have faith?" she replies: "Of course, I am religious, I fulfill my duties. Why ask me that? Are you making fun of me?" And the old man comments in his journal: "That is exactly what all my life I have hated most, just that: for what is it but a coarse caricature, this mediocre employment of the Christian life?" Mauriac is equally pitiless towards the crass and self-complacent bourgeois, whose desires are limited by a well-rounded paunch, a comfortable income, a family to fall back upon in case of need, and the opportunity to indulge in his favorite occupations. He likewise attacks the tyrannical bourgeois family with its narrow-minded bigotry, its attempt to control the private life of its individual members, its censorship of all independence. For example, the father-in-law of the young widow Noémi, in *Le Baiser au lépreux,* makes her his heir on condition that she never remarry.

"Monsieur Jérôme took infinite pride in belonging to a family where the widows never left off their mourning, and so too the other members of this clan manifested great zeal in maintaining Noémi in her entombment."

Mauriac believes that innate in man is some taint which may assume various outward forms. The revelation and development of this taint—apt, in his earlier books, to be carnal desire—its corroding and, in the end, fatal effect on a character, form the theme of Mauriac's work. In *Le Baiser au lépreux,* Jean Péloueyre is cursed with a hideous body, and when he attempts to satisfy his physical passion, he only further repels his young wife: "Noémi, in her long nightgown, used to recite her prayer before the stars. Her bare feet loved the cold tiling; she offered her soft neck to the compassion of the night. She never dried the tear which rolled near her mouth, but drank it. The crickets which crackled at the edge of their holes reminded her of her lord and master. One evening, stretched out upon her sheets, she sobbed, at first almost silently, then with long moans, moved to pity at the sight of her chaste body, as yet intact, but burning with life and vegetal freshness. What would the cricket make of it? She knew that he had the right to every caress, even to that mysterious, terrible one, after which a child would be born, a little Péloueyre all black and sickly. The cricket? She would have it all her life and even in her bed-sheets." *Le Fleuve de feu* is a narration of the void which follows the satisfaction of desires: "We never find that body which we hoped to find." *Le Désert de l'amour,* the story of an unrequited passion, further emphasizes the isolation of the soul even in love. Throughout his work, Mauriac assumes that passion and love are unclean and bestial. He speaks of "the ineffaceable defilement of the wedded union." When a young man, in *Le Nœud de vipères,* seeks to rejoin his wife, the furious old father-in-law inscribes in his diary: "Like a cat entering through a window, he has stealthily penetrated into my house, attracted by the odor." For to Mauriac, passion is not transfigured by the married state.

Whatever blemish man possesses Mauriac believes has been present since early childhood. In opposition to this inherent stain are portrayed the constant swirl of emotions, of habits, prejudices, and desires. Man has no unity in himself, nor can he acquire any in this unceasing turmoil. The logical result is that he must remain as enigmatic to himself as to others. As an epigram for the title-page of *Le Nœud de vipères,* Mauriac quotes from Saint Theresa of Avila: "God, take into consideration that we do not understand ourselves, that we do not know what we want, and that we are always wandering farther away from that which we desire."

Moving in a sphere of complete isolation, Mauriac's characters find that every attempt to seek aid or consolation only emphasizes their utter solitude. He has vouchsafed them no understanding friend, no sympathetic parent to relieve the burden, no wife or husband to share confidences or troubles. The doctor Courrèges, in *Le Désert de l'amour,* hoping for solace from his wife, asks her for the first time in years to walk in the garden with him, but she only speaks of her quarrels with the servants, and reproaches him for forgetting to turn out his light.

There is no refuge from this conflict and isolation except in final defeat and resignation, no oblivion except in a living death or death itself. Noémi, entombed in the family life, "recognized that her fidelity to her dead husband (whom she had never loved), would be her humble glory and that it was her duty not to seek to avoid this obligation." Irène, dying as a suicide, thinks of the empty lives she is leaving behind; she has a presentiment that in continuing to live "there perhaps exists another form of renunciation, another night, another death than this she had sought and desired." (*Ce qui était perdu.*) These men and women, who from lack of faith live in an atmosphere devoid of light, have been analyzed by Marcel Arland as "people who believe themselves to be alone because they are not loved or do not love themselves; let love come and they feel equally alone. Thwarted beings who seek each other with arms deprived of hands, with eyes that cannot see; if they do succeed in reaching one another, it is only to wound each other and themselves."

Mauriac's specialty is to render the sinner more attractive than the so-called righteous man. The more unworthy the character, the more it endears itself to him. "I am like a severe schoolmaster," he writes, "who has all the trouble in the world not to have a secret preference for the inferior nature, rather than the soul so good that it is no longer capable of reacting. Alas! we novelists have this misfortune that inspiration takes its source in the least noble, the least purified of our being, in all that which subsists in us in spite of our better selves. People used to say to me 'Paint virtuous characters.' I replied, 'But I always miss the mark with virtuous ones.' They then would say, 'At least, try to raise the moral level.' But the more I strove to do so, the more obstinately my characters refused to lend themselves to any sort of grandeur."

Destins is the work which aroused the most adverse criticism from the Catholics. It is the novel which brought forth from the amused Gide the accusation that Mauriac was striving to pass as a Christian without being obliged to burn his books. One suspects that in the character of the self-righteous Pierre, Mauriac is disclosing his secret distrust of those who lead a spiritual life in the narrow acceptance of the word. Pierre's dictatorial intervention in the lives of others results only in disaster for all concerned. Mauriac evidently intends that the reader's real sympathies shall go to the unfortunate Bob, who in spite of a licentious life repents and dies in the faith. Likewise, in *Thérèse Desqueyroux,* the story of a woman who attempts to poison her husband, Mauriac ranges himself on the heroine's side: his interest is concentrated, if not on the establishment of Thérèse's innocence, at least in the palliation of her conduct. "The hero of *Le Nœud de vipères* and Thérèse, the poisoner, as horrible as they are," writes Mauriac, "are free at all events from that one vice which I hate most: self-satisfaction. They are not content with themselves, and recognize their misery; and the humble soul is always beloved of God."

It soon becomes apparent that Mauriac spends a great deal of his time and talent evoking the pleasures he expects his readers to condemn. If he is resentful of Mammon's sway, he is also fascinated by it. Not that Mauriac's characters are permitted a lusty sinful time to be atoned for later by suffering and repentance. On the contrary, these people undergo such tortured consciences and moral discomfort that even in the act of sinning, their stolen ephemeral moment is robbed of all pleasure. Mauriac's treachery was to idealize and beautify carnal desire only to condemn it as a snare and delusion. Or as Edmond Jaloux has phrased it: "Mauriac makes us think of a young Levite who accompanies his martyr to some evil place, but not always to protect him." Can it be that Mauriac is a Christian in just so far as a feeling of guilt adds piquancy to his scenes of love? "That anguished conscience," writes Gide, "which lends such charm to your features, and gives so much savor to your writings, must gratify immensely those among your readers who, though abhorring sin, would be annoyed if they were no longer obliged to concern themselves with it. And you know, my dear Mauriac, that in such a case the doom of literature would be sounded, and you are not sufficiently a Christian to give up writing. Your great art is to make accomplices of your readers. Your novels are less calculated to convert sinners than to recall to Christians the existence on earth of something more than Heaven."

Mauriac excels in painting sensual pictures, and this is the one talent his faith enjoins him not to exercise. If to be acclaimed a Christian author is the goal of his desire, it is easy to understand his qualms and misgivings. He may well ask himself what his work has accomplished for the cause of Christianity. At most, he has shown the insufficiency of lives deprived of God. The invariable failure of any two of his characters to attain a mutual and permanent harmony may be one method of decrying a lack of faith. The reader, being supplied solely with negative examples, can only surmise the happy results of righteous living. A few positive illustrations would undoubtedly have pleased his Catholic brethren better. Love and emotion are not lacking in his books, but these are invariably aroused by earthly idols. In most cases their faith reveals itself as little more than a cloak to hide the real nature of their desires, and these, when analyzed, bear a disconcerting resemblance to ordinary physical love. After reading Mauriac it is equally impossible either to blame him for representing evil as victorious or praise him for causing good to triumph. The objections of his Catholic friends can be readily understood. They find his analysis of passion too keen and sympathetic, his depiction of the world too alluring. On the one hand, reproaches from the Church for undermining morals; on the other, sarcasms from the Gides, whom Mauriac is equally loath to displease. No wonder his exasperated critics cried: "Where do you stand?"

Whether Mauriac has merely capitulated before the unremitting onslaught of the Church, or whether his religious convictions have really strengthened, he has finally adopted a more deferential attitude towards Catholicism. In his most tormented moments he never lost his faith, and now, even though a sinner, he has decided to remain a Catholic. So, in a third phase, coincident as it is supposed to be with his conversion, Mauriac says he is striving to purify his art by first purifying his life.

This change of attitude becomes apparent in 1930 with the

publication of *Ce qui était perdu*. In view of the novels which follow it and which strike a more conclusive chord, this earlier work may be called transitional. The stamp of Catholic approval was reserved for *Le Nœud de vipères,* which appeared in 1932. Here the habitual weak and erring character appears, but for the first time Mauriac refuses to be the sponsor of his guilt. Far from casting a halo about the sinner as in his former books, he now portrays the transgressor in all his abject reality, and demonstrates the misery of lives deprived of God. At last there is a seeming accord between the Christian and the novelist, and since Mauriac now condemns where once he condoned, since he has "purified his source," has "sterilized his instrument," he need no longer fear lest the Church will look askance. *Le Nœud de vipères* is the story of a man who has grown old without experiencing that love which has always been the secret craving of his life. His mercenary wife and children, professedly devout Christians, neglect and despise him; they thus foster the worst tendencies in his nature, already miserly and warped. The scant affection and praise he unexpectedly receives are the softening factors which finally lead to his conversion, but this occurs, unfortunately, only upon the eve of his death. Meaning us to cast the blame upon the pharisaical Christians who tormented this unhappy and misguided man, Mauriac says: "How many among us repulse the sinner and thus prevent his arriving at the truth. Truth which because of us can no longer glimmer through!" By causing his sinners to redress their lives and turn towards God, Mauriac became for once the fully ordained, the exemplary Catholic novelist.

Likewise in his next work, *Le Mystère Frontenac* (1933), Mauriac continued to adopt a conciliatory attitude towards the Church. Granting his characters a refuge before defeat and death, he inspires them with a desire to continue the fight. The "mystère" is this family with its many traditions and common weaknesses. Stressing the peace and beauty of self-renunciation, he portrays the mysterious bonds which unite the various members of the family group. Instead of plunging these people into complete moral isolation, as in his earlier manner, he now cements the solidarity of the living, and binds the living to their ancestors. Mauriac's interest has always centered on the four walls of the home, and he is one of the few French novelists today who depicts his characters in relation to their families. Hence the significance of the numerous brothers, sisters, aunts, and cousins who throng his pages.

Those Catholics, however, who hoped that the old demon was dead in Mauriac, must have been chagrined by his recent novel, *La Fin de la nuit* (1935), for it is still evident that his early delectation in portraying the ravages of sin is still lurking within him. As if anticipating the angry storm of protest which might greet this work, and seeking to justify his apparent backsliding, he makes this prefatory statement: "For the reader who wishes, and with reason, that every literary work should mark some spiritual ascension, and who may perhaps be astonished that I should make a new descent towards hell, it is important to recall that the heroine of this book belongs to a former period of my life, and that she is the token of a disquietude I no longer feel." This heroine is none other than the criminal and unregenerate Thérèse Desqueyroux, now pictured at Paris in the abject solitude of her decline, fifteen years after her attempt to kill her husband. Constantly reminded that her sinister mission is to poison the existence of all those who come in contact with her, she nevertheless strives to break the curse by heroically rejecting the advances of a young man, her daughter's fiancé, who for some unaccountable reason has conceived a fatal passion for her. She accomplishes her purpose so far as to force her youthful admirer to marry her daughter, although her sacrifice by no means guarantees the happiness of this young couple. The book ends with Thérèse, stoical but unconverted, awaiting death, that end to the "night" of life. Like a willfully disobedient child, Mauriac once more casts a fearful glance towards his Catholic critics. "Why did I finish Thérèse's story," he writes in his preface, "before she became fully pardoned and bathed in the peace of God? To tell the truth, I did write those consoling pages only to tear them up: I couldn't conceive clearly that priest who should receive Thérèse's confession." Is it bait, concession, or remorse that makes Mauriac go on to say that he will some day find that priest and bury Thérèse in all due odor of sanctity.

However, if Mauriac is still the apostate Christian novelist, he did yield on one important point. Stripping his story of all voluptuous trimmings, he has adhered to the strictest chastity in the love scenes of La Fin de la nuit. But the fact remains that he has chosen the theme of illicit love, with the result that all he portrays is a war of unconvincing passions in which the actors are torn by every conceivable emotion except the logical one of love. In all Mauriac's books, there is no better demonstration of the risks confronting the vacillating Christian novelist, and unless he decides whether to be a good sinner or a good Catholic, he will lose both Paradise and Parnassus.

Mauriac may be unaware of the net value of his conscience, but his chronic moral dilemma has been most remunerative. The appearance of a new Mauriac novel is always a literary sensation, and a part of the curiosity aroused is attributable to his notoriety as a belligerent Roman Catholic. I do not suggest that he seeks publicity at such a price; I only wonder why he has so consistently added fuel to the flame. There can be no doubt as to his sincerity when he says that he has suffered. But where a truly sensitive man would have shrunk from displaying his spiritual difficulties, Mauriac has revealed the drama of his soul in a long series of autobiographical pamphlets, which have had a most consoling market.

This mania for thrusting religion into his work at any cost has left its mark upon his work. Since he claims that no less a matter than the salvation of his soul is at stake, he tinges his novels with an intense, and perhaps to many, a mock-heroic coloring. His stories, floating as they do in a distilled moral atmosphere, become so many vehicles to illustrate his own bitterness and grievances. Unlike a Dickens or a Flaubert, he is unable to put himself outside his work; nor does he show any curiosity about situations foreign to his own potential experience. Because of this, his characters at times lack variety and density of individual life; they make less impression on the reader than the problem they serve to dramatize. However, being mirrors of Mauriac's own warm emotional nature, they reflect, even the most inferior of them, some element of that distinctive personality.

It is not as a moralist, but as a sensualist that Mauriac discloses his richest creative vein. Life for him is a synthesis of every sensation, and he is keenly alert to smell, taste, touch, and sound. In the tiny book of *Le Baiser au lépreux* the sense of smell is introduced in some eighteen passages: medicines, preserved fruits, rye bread, soap balls, clean linen, seaweed, moldy wood, and moist, decaying grapes. He is extremely responsive to the shrill chirping of the cricket, the croaking of the frog, the song of the nightingale, the train rumbling over a viaduct, and above all, the crowing of the cock, as persistent in Mauriac as a *leit-motif* in a Wagnerian opera. Permeated by these sounds and odors, redolent of fragrant pines and vineyards scorched by a torrid sun, his stories vibrate with all the aromatic pungency and animal pulsation of the Gascon moorlands. However, he makes of this living background more than a mere pictorial setting; imbuing his characters with the atmosphere which surrounds them, he relies on their sensory impressions to suggest their states of mind, their emotions, or their actions. Thus, to describe the elation of the youthful Yves, just informed that his poems have been accepted by the *Mercure de France,* he writes: "Three or four scattered drops of rain and finally a steady shower streamed gently down. Yves was conscious of its freshness in his breast; and he was as happy as the foliage in this bursting of the clouds." In the opening scene of *Le Baiser au lépreux,* he paints vividly the spell of utter silence which reigns in the house of a hypochondriac, where even the hinges of the doors have been oiled. In *Génitrix,* each creak and crack of the old house emphasizes the empty loneliness of the lives of its inhabitants. In *Le Nœud de vipères,* an old man is just about to accede to his wife's wishes that he abandon his threatened departure, when in crossing the terrace he notices a semi-circle of chairs and strewn cigarette stubs, mute evidence of a family war-council from which he has been excluded. Mauriac interprets traits of character and emotion by physical peculiarities and habits: Marie Cross lies extended on a sofa with a book she never finishes; Thérèse is perpetually smoking cigarettes; Bernard's fingernails are never clean. One of his most frequent and skilful devices for plot development and character analysis is the use of reminiscence on the part of the protagonist. By means of this adroit linking of the present with the past, the reader comes into direct contact with both, and has the vantage point of a full perspective. *Le Nœud de vipères* is the most striking example of this method. Here an old man, looking back upon his early struggles with his wife and children, writes the story in his journal. Since the family conflict continues to exist, since the personalities who figured in his early life still move about him and substantiate his story, the author creates an atmosphere of intense reality in which the hero moves and breathes, a living man. Mauriac's style being essentially lyric, we penetrate into the inner consciousness of his characters through the rich psalmody of their mental monologues.

For brevity, that preëminent virtue, he has set new standards. Within the economic limits of a short story he concentrates the essence of a complete novel. However, he is not a writer to be read lightly or swiftly. His highly charged style demands the closest attention. To skip a line, a word sometimes, may mean losing a necessary *nuance,* or perhaps the whole coloring of his thought. One element of this elliptical style is his preference for suggestion over direct statement. Partial to oratorical questions and exclamatory sentences, Mauriac resorts to every device to avoid monotony and rigid exposition. Frequently he alters the rhythm of his prose by a daringly displaced adverb or phrase, thus bringing his reader to a halt and obliging him to unravel the sentence structure. This freshens and vivifies his style and imparts to it the charm of poetry. Steep all this in the languorous torpor of a summer day, the Mauriac hour *par excellence,* and it will never occur to you to reproach him for what he may be doing to your soul!

Pierre MacOrlan

TEN years before the World War, a young man of twenty or thereabouts tried his hand in *Le Rire* and other comic periodicals at making people laugh. Life had already taught him that there was not much to laugh about, and indeed his laughter had a decidedly diabolic ring. No stranger to poverty and hardship, he was chiefly concerned with getting enough to eat and a place to sleep. In *Villes,* a book of autobiographical sketches, MacOrlan tells how in these early days he was often obliged to sleep in the haystacks which still existed in the Montmartre of 1900, and how his term of military service was an oasis of comparative ease and comfort. It is therefore easy to believe him when he says that his principal motive in writing was to make money, and that his interest in the Arts was largely inspired by the chance they offered of financial independence. He felt no more inclination to be merry than the unfortunate people in one of his early stories, *Le Rire jaune,* where Europe is shown as the prey of a strange epidemic which exterminates most of its inhabitants in paroxysms of uncontrollable and mirthless laughter. There is an equally grotesque calamity in *La Bête conquérante,* when a worn and vitiated civilization, having discovered how to make pigs talk, is conquered and overrun by its porcine pupils.

MacOrlan had tried his hand at every trade, from proof reading to road digging, before—under a Scottish pseudonym, his real name being Dumarchais—he finally turned to writing. If hunger is responsible for his literary career, it may also be held guilty for that distrust and fear of life which was to be his distinguishing mark. In order to reconcile himself to the pains of living, MacOrlan was obliged to close his eyes and reopen them on some preferred absurdity. This instinct for substitution accounts for his vein of burlesque and caricature, which his subsequent experience in the War only tended to emphasize.

The state of unrest in which war and materialism had plunged the world—the *"système nerveux modèle 1924"* of which Mac-Orlan speaks—had driven most writers into an attitude of negation. Confronted with a civilization stripped bare of beauty and ideals, the poets and dreamers were either entirely chilled by this aridity or found their work profoundly modified by it. Instead of peaceful dreams they had nightmares; hence MacOrlan's macabre and apocalyptic visions. If the order of the day was to flee as far as possible from a universe at war and dominated by machines; if, as most thinkers agreed, the exterior world had proved a complete failure, many writers concentrated on the single reality which survived this wreckage, and studied the individual. Morand and others resorted to travel. Giraudoux and his school found it possible to invest life with new and fanciful beauty. MacOrlan's solution for avoiding chronic melancholia was to escape to the more bizarre regions of the imagination where anything is possible, and there indulge in adventure dreams.

However, as we learn from his piquant *Petit Manuel du parfait aventurier,* the term "adventure" held for him a special meaning, and like Humpty Dumpty's word "incomprehensibility," could be extended to include almost everything. It might be war; it might be business; it might be the mere fact of being born. Is not the fatherland, he asks, the century-old adventure of a single group? Drawing a distinction between two sorts of adventurers, he demonstrates the immense superiority of the passive type. To him the active adventurer seems almost a fool, devoid of both imagination and sensibility. Without the stay-at-home, he would be shorn of all significance. To take one example, MacOrlan believes Captain Kidd's only justification for having lived was the book Marcel Schwob wrote about him some two hundred years later. He argues that the annoying realities accompanying adventure destroy its charms and beauty. This was the experience of Jean Bogaert, one of his characters, a sailor who detested the sea, his vicarious delight derived from books. "Poring over the exploits of some illustrious adventurer, he chose the essential elements which he considered worthy—if only intellectually worthy—to be lived. As a result of a real and exhausting voyage from Brindisi to Tripoli, from Tripoli to Constantinople, the young sailor finally abandoned the sea where he failed to acquire any particular knowledge on the famous study of man." (*La Cavalière Elsa.*) The true lover of adventure in MacOrlan's eyes is the sedentary man, who is wise enough to let others act while he sits back and watches the fun. This type of man abhors movement, brutality, butchery, firearms, and all forms of dangerous activity; yet, in his study, he evokes these things with understanding sympathy and enjoyment. Not every man can become a writer, for which the world should be grateful. But anyone can become a passive adventurer, and it is for this fireside hero that MacOrlan prepares his choicest *mises-en-scène*. With all the persuasive methods of modern advertising, he guarantees to the twentieth-century man a world of fascinating experiences. Since the only worthwhile and absorbingly interesting reality is that conceived by the intelligence and projected in a book, it may be experienced without so much as stirring from the cozy fire and easy chair.

This is where MacOrlan himself elected to remain. After four years at the front, he was only too glad to stay at home. His spirit of adventure was still actively alive, but it was accompanied by an irresistible desire for comfort. So, in his peaceful country retreat, surrounded by orchards and chicken coops, he conjures up the most horrible sea calamities, visits in imagination the sailor's brothel, and evokes the fatigue of the African legionary as he toils ant-like over the burning sands. He found phonograph records sufficient stimulus for his military rhythm, photographs adequate reminders of some evil-smelling port with its black and oily water. Often he has actually witnessed the scenes he describes, and for *La Bandéra,* his story of the Spanish legion, he made a trip to Africa. However, this initial documentation is merely the ground from which his Pegasus leaps, and if he introduces elements of the real, it is only as a springboard for his fancy.

He emerged from the War a practically unknown writer of thirty-four whose modest literary baggage consisted of a few short tales. Writers who, as combatants, had experienced what MacOrlan describes in *Poissons morts,* his book of war impressions, had naturally acquired a realistically brutal conception of life. MacOrlan's personal knowledge of these horrors undoubtedly strengthened the inherent grimness of his nature, and if his books reek of blood and murder, it is because such fearful visions returned spontaneously to a mind fascinated by scenes of terror and repulsion. Where writers such as Giraudoux strove to inhale certain delicate perfumes, MacOrlan "sniffs the rank odors only." When, for example, MacOrlan describes a tree, we may expect him to hang a corpse in its lacy foliage. When it is a Mediterranean city, he stresses not so much the fact that red flowers bloom there, as that the sun makes them rot "like beefsteaks in a giant garbage-can." His early absurdities and boisterous humor were toned down in time, but never entirely renounced. With maturing years, MacOrlan utilized this robust humor to reveal his inner feelings and many sound truths. Inspired by an acute sense of the irony of life is his picture of the murderer forced to bleed for an entire army, his blood finally being capitalized when it yields five million litres. Since this bleeding proceeds on the same gigantic scale as the making of munitions, MacOrlan suggests that it would be twice as useful.

Underneath the disillusioned ex-soldier in MacOrlan lies the artist, for it is impossible to read his books without discovering the painter. In *Villes,* we learn that painting was one of many resources during those poverty-stricken days in Montmartre when he was the intimate of Picasso and other moderns. If, as he confesses, he was never a good painter, in exchanging the brush for the pen he at least retained the artist's observant eye. Bestowing on the artificial a love which nature failed to inspire, he welcomed art as a means of transforming the dull and insignificant into something vital. He views a street, a port, or a landscape not so much from the standpoint of one who is moved by their inherent beauty as from that of the connoisseur who knows which artist would have enjoyed painting them, or how a scenario director would have reproduced them in a studio. That is why his moons rise, his characters embrace, in *"attitudes très carte postale";* why he sees London only as a potential film, and why everything he touches has such an obviously painted look. To say nothing of his impressionistic and highly visual technique, he is apt to amplify or even entirely supplant the description of a landscape by labeling it "a Florentine fresco," or "an earlier William Busch." He compares the white dress and red hair of his Marguerite de la Nuit, silhouetted against some electric street-sign, to a painting by Cézanne; his Elsa reminds him of the shopgirls of the cartoonist Gavarni; while he immediately thinks of Rembrandt when he sees sunrays filtering through a curtain. Is it because snow is so white and blood so red that they figure conspicuously in his stories? Blood shed on snow is even more to his fancy, just as his preference is for red-haired heroines. Frequently resorting to color as a vehicle for sensation, what curious effects he produces with his "red and green in perverse spots," or his "pinks violent and pure"! There is a perfect orgy of color in *La Cavalière Elsa* where the Soviet leaders make decoration an important public work, utilizing it as an instrument to incite revolution, transform the world, and camouflage their crimes. "If we wish to remain conquerors, we must conceal the very forests under canvases painted by our most resolute artists and richly splotched with decorative animals." *"Décoratif"* is the most recurrent adjective in MacOrlan's vocabulary.

But above all else, MacOrlan is a product of his library. Like one of his own heroes, we may picture him in a little room overlooking the Seine, "his sleepless hours haunted by the symbolical flags of the pirates whose exploits are related in the volumes heaped around him, his agile imagination evoking with the most absolute precision the evening battles off the coast of Vera Cruz, its decorative gallows and the riotous life of its exotic dives." For books, as MacOrlan explains, "influence our acts, our gestures, our pains and pleasures. Life would be inconceivable without them. All that man invents, loves, or despises, corresponds to the influence of one or more books adapted to the humor of the individual." To select only a few of his references to authors—the complete list would make a formidable bibliography—his favorite writers are Kipling, Stevenson, Villon, Defoe (*Moll Flanders*), Johnson (*Lives of English Pirates*), Marcel Schwob, Hearn (*Japanese Fairy Tales*), Mallarmé, Hardy (*Tess*), and Conrad, whom he met in Rouen. Whether or not MacOrlan and James Branch Cabell were familiar with each other's works, they have undoubtedly many points in common. Both are highly imaginative anti-realists who reveal a macabre turn of mind, a brutal literary eroticism and a sense of the futility of life. They both seek escape through illusion and dreams of high-handed adventurers of legendary or bygone times just as both are well informed on sorcery and the activities of the Devil.

On MacOrlan's side it is generally possible to trace the source of his literary inspiration, for the simple reason that he usually mentions it. Thus we know that Joan of Arc is modernized in his Elsa; Marlowe and Goethe are caricatured in *Marguérite de la Nuit;* Manon is reflected in Alice Eglantine; Lewis' *Monk* is imitated in the painting of a romantic cloud; Rhineland legends and medieval cabalists are the documentation for the witchcraft and magic doll in *Malice.* Sometimes his interest centers on a gruesome past, sometimes he borrows elements of this past to season the flatness of the present. But being in spite of everything a product of his age, he surveys the scene through hardened modern eyes that strip the past of all romance and, when confronted with the present, concentrate on its sordid aspects. Prompted by a spirit of contrariety, he invariably twists reality into unreality, unreality into reality. Since to him nothing is more unstable than existing conditions, he believes that what *is not* could very easily *become,* and vice versa. Focusing his attention on the lowest types of humanity, he suggests the idea that the outcast of society may only too readily become the norm. This offers a partial explanation for the selection in his earlier books (*Le Chant de l'Equipage,* 1918; *A bord de l'Etoile-Matutine,* 1920; and others) of a world of pirates, soldiers, sailors, thieves and cutthroats of all sorts—the name "jailbird" would honor most of them—who generally meet a violent death either on the gallows or at one another's hands. Although for most of these stories he sought inspiration in the buccaneering world of the sixteenth and seventeenth centuries, only in his imagination could have been born so many frightful murders, garrotings, gibbets, pests and rapes. When he turns to the modern world (*Bob bataillonnaire; Les Pirates de l'Avenue du Rhum; Le Quai des brumes; Dinah-Miami; Quartier réservé; La Bandéra; Nuits aux bouges; Filles d'amour et Ports d'Europe*), he concentrates on prostitutes, policemen, rum runners, and criminals. Witchcraft and sorcery proved an additional source of interest, and in another series (*Le Nègre Léonard et Maître Jean Mullin; Malice; Marguérite de la Nuit*), he became the exponent of various forms of satanism and demonology.

In spite of the fact that as a passive adventurer MacOrlan was able to hand-pick his ruffians, ex-convict soldiers, and sorcerers, he neglected this opportunity to ignore the drab and ordinary run of human beings. Far from imitating the romantic scoundrels of Stevenson, MacOrlan is careful to rob his heroes of every vestige of the picturesque. He utilizes folk-lore and myth, but, handled by him, they are no more poetic than the popular belief that red-haired people are endowed with erotic natures and supernatural powers. He lends an attentive ear to the vernacular in speech and song, but aside from the beautiful prisoner in *Etoile-Matutine,* who with her singing carries her pirate captors back to their childhood and Never-Never Land, these ditties rarely rise above the level of the "Yes, we have no bananas" of *Marguérite de la Nuit*. Although for MacOrlan, the Flying Dutchman still wanders over the twentieth-century seas; Mephistopheles bargains in souls; and the Witches' Sabbath continues its unholy rites—phenomena which he introduces into modern Europe calmly and without apology—in his disillusioned hands the phantom crew becomes transformed into coarse brutes lacking all mystery, the Dutchman himself is a specimen of decayed gentility, while Georges Faust differs from his illustrious ancestor and prototype in procuring Marguérite from a Montmartre street.

Le Nègre Léonard et Maître Mullin is one of the best illustrations of this method. Here the narrator of the story, a sportsloving country gentleman, has employed as his housekeeper and mistress a young woman named Katje, who on her free nights plays a third and secret rôle of sorceress. The discovery of this last talent is due to her master's hunting dog, which one morning at dawn finds her naked in a thicket, having missed, we suppose, the last aerial broomstick. This seems the right moment to speak of the dogs in MacOrlan, for a number appear in his stories, and they are always sensitive to the supernatural. Since there is a great deal of the supernatural, their rôle is a prominent one. In *Nègre Léonard,* the dogs dislike this servant-witch intensely. In *La Vénus internationale,* it is a little foxhound which senses danger and warns his masters when the wild animals begin their strange migration. The uniform breed of these dogs, usually terriers, gives the impression of one dog, probably MacOrlan's own. Or is this just another one of his tricks, like Katje's mop of flame-colored hair? This mysterious heroine, her double life exposed, induces her employer to accompany her to a Witches' Sabbath. As a newcomer he is properly introduced, and after hearing the Black Mass, falls easily into conversation with the Goat-Devil's two henchmen, Léonard and Jean Mullin, who complain that crime and the motives for crime have deteriorated in quality. The hero discovers for himself that the revelers' interests are limited in the main to lust and money, and that the face of the master has a weary look. Later he witnesses the further decline of the Devil's prestige when his modern disciples' increasing indifference to sin has shorn him of all glamour, and has reduced him from a powerful god to an insignificant he-goat in a stable. After Katje dies, and Léonard becomes a dancer, and Jean Mullin, appropriately enough, a magistrate, the world is left irremediably good, and thus goes to ruin for lack of imagination.

In *La Cavalière Elsa* (1922) and *La Vénus internationale* (1923), MacOrlan emerges from the jealously guarded domain of his library to speculate on the future, and to prophesy catastrophe and revolution. In *La Cavalière Elsa,* he chooses an indefinite period when the World War has already become a confused memory, and projects a purely intellectual concept of the invasion of Europe, and of France in particular, by the Soviet army. He believes that the masses, fundamentally sentimental, have always needed a mystic figure to fire their imagination. The Machine Age has changed the mode of living but not the mentality of the people who, deprived of their ancient but now obsolete symbols, have never been supplied with new ones. Comparing the proletariat to a woman dying from the suppression of her tenderness and reduced to playing "mother" to a doll salvaged from an old trunk, the shrewd Soviet leaders propose to find another doll, a modern Joan of Arc, some vague literary personality calculated to inspire a new religious feeling and a new sentimentality. The heroine of this redeemer legend will serve as a symbol for whatever the soldiers most want to find: an aristocrat, a prostitute, a nun, a sister, or a mother. Elsa, a beautiful young Jewess, in private life the least of saints, is selected as this mystic goddess. "Remember Joan of Arc," the Russian leader says. "She passed almost unperceived among her contemporaries. All legendary figures should be of this variety. Later, when people shall ask who was this Elsa, martial maid, no one must be able to recall a single feature of her face, not one of her familiar gestures, even the color of her hair." Blood being the daily drink of the passive adventurer, it is necessary for the Cavalière to shed a few drops at the beginning of her career. With such a leader, and garbed in fantastic uniforms, the Red Army passes the frontiers unopposed and takes possession of Paris. Here the conspirators count on maintaining their prestige by organizing lavish entertainments. "Distribute gold profusely," is the order of the day, "and decorate the world with the most brilliant colors you can find: frescoes, figures, Chinese lanterns, cockades, and oriflammes. Mobilize all the mechanical pianos and teach young boys and girls to sing choruses, so that upon the broadcasting of the signal, their hymn may be heard simultaneously throughout the world." The leader of the Reds must do his part as well, and to prove his capacity as a superman devours an entire cow of sugar before the awe-struck citizens. But the soldiers, their services no longer needed, revert automatically to their peaceful, middle-class instincts, and build cottages along the Marne. In representing the revolutionists as settling down to commonplace security, MacOrlan evidently wishes to show that man may be led to the waters of pure adventure, but cannot be made to drink. And so, in this grimly humorous caricature of the future world, MacOrlan shows that civilization will finally degenerate into a prolonged street fair of petty fireworks. With the intelligentsia asleep and the masses coarsened by crass indulgence, life will be reduced to an obscene and humdrum brawl. More, however, than a pessimistic apocalyptic vision, *La Cavalière Elsa* discloses its author, although of plebeian birth himself, disliking and fearing the common people. While free from snobbery, as an intelligent man, he cannot help regarding the masses as philistines. When he personifies the soul of Russia in the sordid Elsa, its brain and arm in the Clown, its king in the People, a king, however, with grease and machine oil under his fingernails, MacOrlan does not satirize a single nation, but merely stresses the absurdity and futility of all revolutions. This curious story, probably his nearest approach to a completely successful book, is strongly imprinted with his memories of the War and the philosophies of a period when skepticism ruled the day. A revolution is of profit to someone, but what matters it to whom? Composed with all the grotesque movement, fantasy, incoherence, and glitter of a great modernistic ballet, as a novel it will doubtless become as obsolete as the life it ridicules, to resume its historic value in a later century when, like some museum piece, it may inspire the liveliest curiosity.

La Vénus internationale is placed at a still more vaguely outlined future period when the cultural disintegration of Europe is complete. It is the age when intellectual pursuits have fallen into such disrepute that university professors and intellectuals of every description have formed themselves into disorderly nomadic bands, to escape starvation by raiding the countryside. The book was written in a post-war period when the peasants were in a fair way to become the richest class in France, and this perhaps suggested the idea that they would some day rule the world. Although in his country home MacOrlan is reported to be on friendly terms with his peasant neighbors, he has no illusions in their regard, and neglects no occasion to remark upon their inferior intelligence. His low opinion of proletarian psychology is revealed by representing the picturesque life and clear vision of former days as having given way to purely materialistic standards. Again it is a vision of the Soviet régime, this time scheming to accustom the masses to the artificial scenery with which Machine Age genius has surrounded them. The beauty of industrialism must be explained to them if they are to feel at home among the new and imposing creations of cement and steel, landscapes composed of smokestacks and railway stations, and "wrought-iron arabesques springing from the ground to replace earth's last sickly tree." Again the leaders have recourse to a beautiful Jewess, this time Claude, who is sent out to disseminate their doctrines through every artery of Europe. Ostensibly she is only peddling cheap merchandise among the peasants; in reality, she is the secret communistic agent intended to sow the seeds of unrest and dissatisfaction. The book ends with the description of the last night of two brothers, the leading characters, as they grope in the dark for matches, their nerves on edge at the howling of the elements, even their dog terrified by the mysterious cosmic forces which threaten just outside the door. This final chapter, one of MacOrlan's greatest artistic moments, predicts a Europe which shall become a barren plain submerged in snow and ice, and invaded by crows and wolves. Comparing the world to a vast operating table where the patients, put to sleep by an unknown anæsthetist, are awaiting the knife of a monstrous surgery, he exclaims: "Adieu! ancient Europe! Sober flower of delicate petals, beautiful corolla broken on its stem!"

Deploring the modern world, and withdrawn to a universe of his own devising, MacOrlan has no hope of a superior civilization. He believes that the world is still in darkness, and until some enlightenment comes, mankind must continue to live in darkness. The attempt to penetrate the veiled forms of this moral night and what he calls "the frozen contours of the psychological mystery enveloping humanity," is the real adventure of his life.

MacOrlan's work is long and unequal, while many of his themes are renewed with monotonous frequency throughout some twenty books. He is not a psychological novelist, and when once the book has been set aside, it is difficult to recall the features of a single character. Even if these puppets of MacOrlan could persuade us of their actual existence, the author is always leaning over their shoulder to call attention to their unreality. Lest we should be misled, he labels each creation and emphasizes the hollowness of his panorama by such qualifying terms as *littéraire, provisoire, intellectuel, décoratif*. He is not primarily interested in character delineation, nor does he vouchsafe a single pleasing figure. Indeed, he is the first to remind us that, if painted truthfully, none of these pirates, scoundrels, and legionary soldiers merit sympathy. For MacOrlan believes that at best the adventurer is only a comic figure, an undecided nature, a moral weakling who is the sport of circumstance. "At the bottom of all adventure," he explains, "is submission of the spirit. That is why my best characters, those at least who interest me the most, are social failures. However, let us not be misled by that. As a literary subject, the unsuccessful man is much richer in possibilities than, let us say, the engineer. For what does the engineer desire of life, what does he need? His course is traced in advance. What could I draw from him? He is well behaved, of good education, happy. Talk to me rather of the man who through some vice, lack of will power, or defective reasoning has failed in all his enterprises. Such a person will never be happy or steady. Inherent in every adventurer are his impulsive and ineffectual movements, his mixture of outward brutality and inner weakness, and this is sufficient to make of him a character of inexhaustible interest."

For all of MacOrlan's literary eroticism, love has little place in his books. His treatment of the Faust theme classes love not as one of the great illusions, but as an easily satisfied appetite. Just as his adventurers are never romantic lovers, so their erotic emotions are reduced to the category of digestive disturbances, unless indeed they are merely indicative of a lack of intelligence. Most of his heroines regard love as a possible incident or byproduct of their ancient and remunerative profession. If it even chances that a character sets some store by love, he or she is invariably the loser thereby.

The individuals in MacOrlan's books are soon forgotten, but not the bloodstream which courses through them. This, to be sure, is a turbid, fetid stream, but it is always vigorous, and its purple fumes contain no poison. In spite of his completely amoral attitude, he can hardly be considered a dangerous influence. His angle of vision is too frankly artificial to reach the soul, much less besmirch it. His scenes of gross sensuality, cruelty, and terror are only offered as mental adventures far removed from life. As an amateur sorcerer playing with alchemy, he invents human demons and poisonous gases but is careful to confine them to a chimerical caldron, and if the Devil leads a mad round of sinners, these unclean spirits must disappear at the crowing of the cock, leaving the countryside none the worse. In spite of disillusion and desolation the gloom is more than offset by his extraordinary vitality and zest, and his robust personality adds a refreshing note of virility to the effete atmosphere so prevalent in contemporary letters. As a fantasist, he has not the light, felicitous touch of Giraudoux, whom at times he appears to imitate, but—rare phenomenon in modern times—here is a writer more interested in external objects than in himself. Despite the foul scenes narrated, MacOrlan is probably less sophisticated than the average reader, and this may be one of the reasons for his popularity.

Valery Larbaud

As Lamartine said a century ago: "Travel means undergoing, a hundred times a year, impressions and emotions which the stay-at-home is lucky to experience in a lifetime. For the enrichment and discipline of both mind and heart, it is the duty of every philosopher, statesman, and poet to be a frequent traveler." If by cosmopolitan is implied the ability to assimilate and enjoy the cultural advantages of other countries, Valery Larbaud is assuredly cosmopolite. Where Stendhal adopts Milan, and Montherlant Spain, Larbaud goes farther and adopts all Europe. Indeed, the blood of Mme de Staël must flow in the veins of this supertraveler, and if Morand and other globe-trotters have recently flooded the world with travelogues, Larbaud may be said to have set the vogue.

He was born and lived for a long time in Vichy, and it is not improbable that this international resort may have played its part in the formation of so catholic a taste. Having begun his never-ending travels at the age of seventeen, he has wandered over every highway and byway of Europe. He has assumed the rôle of a picador at Valencia, a philologist at Uppsala, a nihilist at Cracow, as naturally as that of the scholar and humanist in Paris or in his native home in Allier. It is not surprising that his hobby is to collect lead soldiers, maps, and flags. His library contains twelve thousand volumes classified according to country and bound in the appropriate national colors. For one of his heroes, Barnabooth, he selects a South American, and shifts the scene from Italy to Russia and England. The background for *Fermina Marquez* is a French boarding school, but it is described as being "more cosmopolitan than an international exposition." In *Beauté, mon beau souci,* a Frenchman loves an English girl; in *Amants, heureux amants,* there is a Franco-Norwegian-Italian trio; while in *Mon plus secret conseil,* the young hero, who is a Parisian, will presumably marry the Greek girl whom he has met in Paris. For in Larbaud's books, were a Frenchman to love one of his own countrywomen, it would have a slight savor of incest.

Just as his map of Europe is simplified by the annihilation of all frontiers, his historical perspective is an unbroken line from the Roman Empire to the present day. Impressed by the continuity of nations, social groups, and communities, he has an unusual understanding of the evolution of divergent points of view and customs. If we attribute to him the sentiments of one of his own characters, little Joanny Leniot, he believes most modern ills are the result of the disintegration of the Roman Empire. "Why did Charlemagne permit the division of the Empire? Why did not Charles the Fifth make a new conquest of Gaul? Why did not Napoleon have himself crowned Emperor of the Occident? What is the name of this barbarian tribe to which I belong? I am not French. My catechism tells me I am a Roman Catholic, but I translate this to mean 'Roman' and 'master of the world.'" In like manner, Larbaud considers French, Italian, and Spanish so many bastard dialects derived from Vulgar Latin.

As a "great citizen of Europe," he has broken the chains which bind most of us to a single nationality or community. He calls himself a perpetual "runaway"; hence, free from blind loyalty to any social unit. His attitude towards society, politics, and morality is completely unprejudiced. If he reveals himself as a rebel, it is as an orderly and peaceful one who has no leaning towards anarchy. His tact and good taste permit him to defy propriety with impunity.

It is impossible to conceive Larbaud in a state of boredom. Life holds for him as many sources of interest as there are hours on a time-table. It is obviously Larbaud speaking when Barnabooth from his train window says: "I should like to spend an entire life in each of these little German towns: going on Sundays to chapel; taking part in the local festivities; frequenting the nobility of the region." So whether it be the spectacle of the Florentine housewife lowering her market basket into the street below, or the "soothing beauty of the gentle, indulgent, intelligent Tuscan light," Larbaud finds a never-failing thrill in travel. Far from being a mere pleasure-seeker, Larbaud's exoticism is constructive, and he deliberately absorbs the life of foreign countries to enrich his own personality. Complaining of a certain type of tourist who jeers at foreign oddities, he thinks that to be completely intelligent is to find nothing ridiculous. "Take, for example, Italy. It is not a question of discovering things to say either for or against this country; but rather of things to say *about* it. What an idiot is the person who does nothing but criticize a country! Or that other type who admires everything!" According to Larbaud, being impressed by everything foreign is not a sign of cosmopolitanism, and in the person of Barnabooth he scoffs at an Italian Anglomaniac who could not speak a word of English, yet found everything in his own country dull or base. Barnabooth, therefore, is the first to smile at himself when he attempts to light his cigarette in the Italian manner, or throw his cloak about his shoulders with studied nonchalance. To him those Frenchmen are especially absurd who go to London and affect a British phlegm only to lose it later in the excitement of conversation, and upset their mugs of ale.

As an admirable example of the intelligent cosmopolite, Larbaud learned to speak some half dozen languages (in *Jaune, bleu, blanc,* he tells of his thrills while studying Portuguese) ; assimilated the literatures of twice as many countries; and utilized this knowledge to introduce many unknown writers to his countrymen. He made his literary début with a translation of Coleridge's *Ancient Mariner,* and one of his latest and most charming books, *Ce vice impuni, la lecture,* is a series of essays on William Ernest Henley, Coventry Patmore, Francis Thompson, James Stephens, and Walt Whitman. The first Frenchman to study or translate Samuel Butler, Landor, Chesterton, Conrad, Hardy, Stevenson, Joyce, Ramon Gomez de la Serna, and a host of others, he rendered no less valuable service in presenting Rimbaud, Claudel, Péguy and Giraudoux to the English public. His contributions to English and South American periodicals are written in the language of these countries, while he intersperses his French books with many an Italian, Spanish, and English word.

These books are few in number and usually overlap one another. *Fermina Marquez,* which Larbaud began in 1906 at the age of twenty-five, was only terminated in 1909. *Le Journal de A. O. Barnabooth,* begun in 1902, was not completed until 1912. *Enfantines* was under way in 1908 but not published until 1918. *Amants, heureux amants* appeared in instalments between the years 1916 and 1918. In addition to *Ce vice impuni, la lecture,* his latest books are essays and travelogues collected in *Allen* (1926), *Jaune, bleu, blanc* (1929) and *Technique littéraire* (1932). Writing constitutes a small, though integral part of his life, and is coexistent with other varied interests. These are reflected in his books, which form, in fact, a continuous autobiography, veiled and reticent, as might be expected from an author who claims to write with a mask before his face. His experiences as a frail and almost feminine youth, isolated from the boisterous games of his schoolmates and left dreaming and none too happy in some corner of the playground, will ac-

count for *Enfantines*. The memory of years spent at a boarding
school near Paris, where, as he says, more Spanish was heard
than French, was the inspiration for *Fermina Marquez;* while
A. O. Barnabooth is the echo of his early travels on the continent
with a tutor. It is also quite in the picture that he had some in-
cidental and casual love affairs such as those described in *Amants,
heureux amants.*

Since cosmopolitanism is a luxury reserved for the rich, Larbaud was fortunate in being financially independent. Money
gave him cultural advantages and ample leisure to contemplate
the world and his relation to it. But Larbaud makes of his psy-
choanalysis something more than a diverting and fashionable
game. If Barnabooth, or Larbaud, is self-analytical, his purpose
is to glean some final truth which will serve humanity. He strives
to make his orientation cover every mood and encompass a lifetime. "The only thing which satisfies me today," he writes, "is
to see clearly both within and without myself; not only my adolescent naïveté, for example, but its relationship to the present
moment as I gaze into the depths of this pure Italian light." And
meditating on his youth, he adds: "It was my true self, that
little isolated beam which sought its way beneath the earth before emerging to fuse with the great life of the universe."

One of the reasons his characters are so plausible is because of
his care to trace their evolution from childhood. Frequently he
confines himself to that early period. His subtle and profound
analysis of the child and adolescent is not merely an amused
appreciation of the ingenuousness of the young: it springs
from his respect for youth. Remembering his own early introspection, he attaches the greatest importance to the thought
life of the child. The little figures in *Enfantines* who pass in
review present more than wistful, dreaming faces. Stirred by
emotions as violent as they are at times bitter, their souls are
penetrated with a mysticism not understood, nor even suspected,

by their elders. The dramas of life start early. Whether it be the tiny Milou, cutting his finger in order to wear the same stigmata which disfigure the hand of the little shepherdess he loves; the twelve-year-old Rose Lourdin, suffering all the ravages of an adult passion in her "crush" on another girl; the boy waiting for his music lesson and communing with the face he believes he has discovered in the veins of the marble fireplace; or *Eliane à 14 ans* and her awakening to the call of sex; all these young people reveal an intensity of emotional life rarely equaled, and even more rarely surpassed, in later years. "I have often listened to these great anguishes of childhood," the author writes. "You hear no sob, nothing except, at long intervals, a little whistling sound."

In his analysis of the child, Larbaud stresses the complete mental separation which usually exists between children and parents. "Face," says the little boy in *L'Heure avec la figure,* "I have never told anybody that there was an image in the hearth, and I have kept everyone from looking in your direction. But luckily, grown-up people never see anything anyway." If the children in Larbaud's stories are inclined to feel their superiority over adults, and meet life with simplicity and frankness, it is because they have not yet become the victims of ready-made ideas and prejudices. Larbaud does not say that enmity necessarily exists between the grown-up and the child; in fact, he provides many instances of affection, but he calls attention to the magic line forever separating child and adult.

Fermina Marquez is the story of the ambitions and rivalries of a group of adolescent schoolboys. Into their young lives steps Fermina, a bewitching Colombian girl of sixteen, the sister of one of their schoolmates. She steps out again just as completely, after firing the heart of the megalomaniac Joanny Leniot; of the handsome and hot-blooded South American Santos, whose instincts are purely animal; and finally, the timid little Camille, whose tribute to his beloved is the gift of a diminutive Colombian flag, and whose sobs are stifled under cover of the night.

The book can hardly be called a novel. These young people are thrown, for a moment only, on a magic-lantern screen where their colors and contours are cast in high relief. We should have liked to hear more about the fate of the lovely and enigmatic Fermina, torn as she was between her mystical aspirations and her human love. But like a helpless marionette, she is suddenly jerked out of sight. Did she become a nun or a wife? The pendulum might easily have swung in either direction. The only unifying element in this book may be called the school itself, to which the anonymous teller of the story, a former student, returns in later years. The place has long been abandoned; only an ancient caretaker remains, the sole survivor of its former active life.

The bulk of Larbaud's work antedates the War. In his analysis of Barnabooth, young multimillionaire and poet, the author mirrors not only his own spiritual aspirations, but those of a whole generation of young men who lived between the years 1900 and 1914. The fact that Barnabooth is a South American has no real significance, for he is a European in everything but name. What these vague but ardent yearnings, these alternate impulses towards mysticism and sensuality, this sense of independence and fraternity, this clumsy groping towards the truth; what all these would have become in the normal course of events, it is impossible to imagine. We follow Barnabooth and his friends through their youthful dissipations until we see them knocking for admission at the gates of the traditional. Larbaud abdicates his mentorship when he has brought his characters to the threshold of a presumably useful life. If he had waited one year longer, the brutal determinant of war would have made involuntary heroes of them. To trace the War's effects on the younger generation, we must turn to a later group of writers, such as Morand, Montherlant, Drieu, and others.

Archibaldo Olson Barnabooth—to give the young Peruvian his full name—possesses the imposing income of 10,450,000 pounds. This is not the mere study of a multimillionaire. It is the analysis of a personality struggling against the impediment of wealth. There is fundamentally very little difference between the poor, poor man, such as Duhamel's Salavin, and the poor, rich man, as illustrated by Barnabooth: the salvation of either soul proves equally baffling.

Barnabooth made his first appearance as the author of a tiny volume of free verse, *A. O. Barnabooth, poèmes d'un riche amateur,* which Larbaud published in 1908, that is to say, when both he and his hero were in their twenties. To use the young poet's own words, these are his "bowel-rumblings," in which he not only proclaims himself the "bard of Europe, its railroads, theatres, and constellation of cities," but reveals his anguish as a man. This indefatigable but naïve globe-trotter claims to have first discovered the sweetness of life through the windows of a transcontinental express. Indeed, he knows the world only as viewed from first-class compartments, yachts and sumptuous hotels. "Lend me your great noise, your gentle pace, as you slip by night through illuminated Europe, O *train de luxe!* And the agonizing music which rumbles along your gilt-leather corridors, while behind your lacquered doors with their heavy copper latches, millionaires lie sleeping."

But railway stations, post offices, jewelry shops, luxurious bathtubs and chocolate candies, mingled with more picturesque delights of nearly every countryside and capital of Europe, cannot efface the youthful philosopher's realization of the futile emptiness of life. He describes himself as "a man whom the sense of social injustice and human misery have rendered completely mad. In order to avenge those who are obliged to suffer I wish to plunge myself into still greater suffering than theirs and become the most ignoble of men. But alas! I am too rich. Automatically rendered virtuous through wealth, I am forever denied the privilege of being evil."

Five years later, in Larbaud's long essay-novel, *A. O. Barnabooth,* we find him still searching for what in his youthful pretentiousness he calls "the absolute," and striving to free himself from all social and moral slavery. Barnabooth is a young man in revolt, against just what he and we are never exactly sure. He is by no means a complete picture of the modern man, for, as one critic reminds us: "Larbaud has only chosen princes as his heroes. Young, handsome, intelligent, polyglot, and wealthy, they have everything which should bring them happiness. They forge their own misfortunes, for, with the possible exception of the pangs of love, they could have spared themselves every form of suffering, if their mysticism, their taste for humility, and their idealism, had not poisoned their Epicurean egotism."

If Barnabooth liberates himself from the bondage of material possessions, he is illogical enough to hold on to the money their sale nets him. If, in order to lighten his soul, he travels without baggage, he yet lolls luxuriously in a private *wagon-salon* or engages an entire floor at the Ritz. He is frequently seen casting away his excess clothing in the Arno, but he spends the next hour in the shops replenishing his wardrobe. He tries every device which will place him on a level with the poor, everything, that is, except the simple expedient of giving up his fortune. His moods are as varied as his reactions are unpredictable. He wants to help the poor, but he also despises them; he wishes to make amends to society for the immense wealth which he enjoys, but in selling his property he nearly plunges Europe into a financial panic. Although he pretends to be the most humble of men, he resents the vulgar crowd being admitted to his favorite art galleries. He abhors the abuses of his own caste, but in his effort to debase himself by shoplifting, he sponsors evils no less reprehensible. Bewildered, unsettled, sensitive to every current, he is a fluctuating barometer which usually falls back to average pressure.

Always Barnabooth complains of the ill will and lack of understanding which surround him as a millionaire, for although a man of dreams, enthusiasm, altruism, and talent, the world sees in him only an idler and a grotesque nitwit. "I greet these men of lesser fortune familiarly as man to man. They bow and scrape before me, only, when my back is turned, to stick out their tongues at me. Even in the obsequious manner with which they grasp my hand, I can feel their scorn." So Barnabooth believes himself forever barred from true friendship; his companions are composed of parasites or snobs; and, when not exploited, he is turned into an object of derision.

Remembering the reaction of so many students freshly liberated from their universities, Larbaud depicts his hero's delight in discovering his former teachers' mistakes in judgment. This grudge against his professors is evident throughout the pages of the young man's journal, and Barnabooth comes to the following drastic and impetuous conclusion: "Once again my experience contradicts everything my instructors told me, and I am now of the opinion that the only delicacy of soul is to be found among the rich and great. And what is the wisdom of the older man but the wearing out of the young man's feelings and the cooling of his youthful fervor?"

As might be expected, Barnabooth is idealistic and chivalrous towards women. Not accustomed to such treatment, women are bored by it. His first serious passion is for Florrie Bailey, a music-hall singer and courtesan. To put his theory of humility to its supreme test and to redress in his own person one phase of social injustice, he asks this woman to marry him, only to be rejected.

He learns that marriage is the last thing she desires and that she has been secretly employed by his guardian to keep him out of greater mischief. "No, Barnabooth," says the philosophical Florrie, "we prostitutes have a social mission. We are created for hard-working men who need distraction from their labor; or else for the married man who seeks to forget the dreary face of his wife. The rich young bachelor should not shirk the responsibility of marrying from his own class."

His second love affair is equally ill starred. This time his choice falls upon the opposite extreme, for Gertrude Hansker is an amazonian beauty, rich, intelligent, and magnetic. A chance meeting of the two renews an old romance begun in America years before. The young woman, now married, asks nothing better than to become his mistress, but is unwilling to divorce and marry him. However, a transitory love affair has no appeal for Barnabooth, who has been warned that "liaisons begun in champagne usually end in camomile." "In spite of the fact that everything nowadays pushes one towards such unions," writes the domestic-minded young man, "I want none of that, and once for all, say 'no' to adulterous counsels and sterile love."

He is at the height of his discouragement when his friend Stéphane, a Russian prince, offers him his own solution of such problems: "If it is your wealth which thwarts you, lead your money and do not be led by it. Seek the Christian's ideals and learn to serve humanity. Above all, stop criticizing yourself in this futile manner. Since man cannot escape his origin, why strive to be a superman?" So renouncing his search for the absolute, and admitting his incapacity for assuming uncongenial responsibilities, Barnabooth finally aspires to a comfortable home and a tranquil life; marries a humble Peruvian girl whom he has met in London; and takes passage for his native country. The reader is under no illusion as to how long this moody young man will be content to remain in the depths of South America.

Is not Larbaud secretly smiling at the young bridegroom as he stands among his heaped-up baggage on the quay and hears jangling in his ears the "loro—lorito—lorito" of his wife's parrot?

In spite of the enthusiastic praise usually bestowed on *Beauté, mon beau souci,* the first of the three stories in *Amants, heureux amants,* Larbaud, in choosing an English setting, for once does not seem thoroughly at ease in a foreign atmosphere. However, judging from the American novels of Duhamel, Durtain, and other recent writers, the Anglo-Saxon still remains a mystery to the average Frenchman. Or as Anglo-Saxons, are we unduly jarred when Larbaud's hero, a young Parisian living in London with an English woman of thirty-eight as his housekeeper and mistress, transfers his affections from mother to daughter, a young girl of fourteen? In addition, the story is sentimental and rather cheap, indicating that Larbaud's taste is not infallible. Especially unpalatable is that passage where Marc's growing passion is described in the always deplorable *carte du tendre* method, and is represented as having "left Peaceful Possession for a more hilly region in the Land of Tenderness." Nor, in a lesser matter, is it easy to share the author's enthusiasm for his heroine's name of Queenie, nor for that of her friend Ruby, when he makes his hero say: "Why are certain names so beautiful? Who will explain the charm they have?"

Queenie's history is *roman-feuilleton* at best. Left to her own resources, believing that Marc has abandoned her, the young girl is seduced and abandoned by a second admirer. We follow Queenie from her decision to remain poor but virtuous, to her marriage with a wealthy suitor, who has become, unconvincingly enough, a third victim of her charms, and with whom, apparently, she is to live happily ever after. However, in spite of its lapses into somewhat tawdry bathos, *Beauté, mon beau souci,* has its numerous admirers, not the least of whom is one enraptured French critic who exclaims: "Queenie, Queenie Crosland! Oh, delicious little heroine! Because we first saw you disguised as a white and blue Pierrette, we shall never forget either your charming name, or your dazzling apparition. We stole from you a little bell which we tinkle in our hours of melancholy."

The other two stories in this volume are written in a form of inner monologue, which Larbaud explains is in imitation of James Joyce and Edouard Dujardin, two authors whom he greatly admired. In such a medium, where all barrriers are down, we are taken unreservedly into the narrator's confidence and become imperceptibly identified with the latter's stream of consciousness. In *Amants, heureux amants,* the reader's imagination wanders with the hero from the voluptuous disarray of the bed where the young man contemplates his two mistresses now wrapped in Dionysian slumber and enlaced in each other's arms, to the thought of his absent love, "the mysterious one of whom I think, and whose lingerie, crumpled, could be contained within the fist." From these teeming reveries, swerving as they do from *jeunes filles à marier* to Greek conjugations, the reader gleans that on the following day, the hero will abandon these *femmes damnées* (not, however, because of the relations between these two women, never a dampener to a Frenchman's ardor) to rejoin the one of whom he thinks—or, what seems more likely, to resume the study of his favorite Greek and Latin authors.

"And what if I were to lead her back to her husband?" begins the third and final story, *Mon plus secret conseil.* So muses yet another young man who, sometimes called "I," sometimes "he," is also planning to abandon his mistress, this time a young divorcée whom he has led from Paris to Naples and is now deserting for a Greek girl. Whether he actually performs the deeds of which he talks the reader must conjecture, for reality and imagination are so closely intermingled in the monologist's mind that it is impossible to unravel what is real from what is dream. The incoherent, broken sentences of the last two pages are already charged with the soporific atmosphere of sleep.

Larbaud is now over fifty. Since so far his interest has manifested itself chiefly in children and young people, we may never know how Barnabooth and the others would conduct themselves were they married or under the spell of really adult passion. His young heroes seize present opportunities and transitory loves, and usually seem relieved when these are over. Their minds appear more active than their hearts. They give of both, but only as a loan, which they reclaim with interest. In several cases the sex impulse is motivated more by altruism and curiosity than by passion. For emotional intensity, the odds are in favor of the women, and even more, the children and the adolescent, most of whose yearnings, according to *Enfantines,* are never to be fulfilled.

Vast culture, distinction of tone, and serenity of spirit combine to make Larbaud a writer of unusual charm. He can infuse dreamy glamour through a book like *Enfantines,* distill the subtle aroma of poetry through every page of *Amants, heureux amants,* or with grace and vivacity portray the vacillating Barnabooth. He has not been a prolific writer, and except for his continued activity in translating and promulgating foreign authors, his literary career seems prematurely ended. But however slight in bulk, his work has ever been rare in quality, and with such lines as: "How sad must be that country where no Mass is said—yes, and after the country without Mass, the city which has not seen the sea!" reveals imagination, simplicity, and beauty.

Paul Morand

"MY cheque-book suspended from my neck in a little iron box, I like to set out alone with my traveling bag. Its smooth flanks are like cheeks on which all winds have breathed, all fingers have passed, hotel and station labels, and multicolored customs chalk. Its bottom, which is wearing out, is blue with the sweat of toil, with sea-water, with vomitings, and red where eau de Cologne bottles have cracked inside." So Morand describes his old valise. But more than the realistic painting of a piece of luggage, the valise is at once a symbol and portrait of its owner.

The first label pasted on his bag was in Russia, where his parents were living when Morand was born. At the age of thirteen he was sent to England, and another label bears the stamp of Oxford University. "From the age of seventeen," he writes, "my only study of France was from the point of view of her relationship to other countries; when I studied geography it was that of the world at large; when history, it was diplomatic; when law, international. At the age of twenty, a French treatise on the origins of literary cosmopolitanism exerted a great influence over me and opened new horizons. My first book, which was never published, was inspired by Larbaud's *Barnabooth*. After my military service in France I passed eight years in foreign travel. It was only upon returning from abroad that I began to write in earnest. If cosmopolitanism is to be found in my books, it springs from my life." Morand's subsequent service as a diplomatic attaché in Edinburgh, Munich, London, Rome, and Madrid fostered his inherent *wanderlust*. He tells us that he buys his socks in France, his shoes in America, his shirts in China, his gloves in Italy, his hats in Germany, and his over-coats in Spain. The remaining articles of his dress must be British, for Morand resembles a smartly tailored sportsman, with a touch of the *apache*. Like one of his own heroes who sings a hymn of joy in honor of frontier towns, Morand regards all exits from his country as so many gates to liberty.

As a diplomat and bohemian, Morand was in an excellent position to take the pulse of a shattered and delirious Europe. A part of the routine of his life was to hear the din of cabarets, and to be the guest of many establishments, whether "open" or "closed" at night. Here he heard many a strange tale and con-fession from the human wrecks who frequented them. The commonplace had no attraction for him, and wishing to make a methodical investigation of strange derelicts whom the War had cast adrift, he scoured the haunts of dissipation and vice in quest of his subjects. He sought the wandering, unprotected girl, the drug addict, the degenerate, the social outcast; in short, any human embodiment of moral and intellectual degradation. Dragged as it was through all the dives of Europe, it is small wonder if his bag became soiled and scarred. Although the pulse he counted was undoubtedly authentic, it was never the healthy or normal one, but always the irregular rhythm of debauch and anarchy. "When Morand learns that a revolution is brewing," jeers one French critic, "he rushes to the place to observe it." From these plague spots he brought back many a fantastic tale to convince the humdrum stay-at-homes of his rare and penetrat-ing psychology. Rareness it possessed, but hardly depth, for in confining his choice to extreme and unusual types viewed from violent angles, Morand was merely reporting what only too glaringly struck the eye.

With his curiosity about life, his genius for taking brilliant flashlights, his ability to capture in a few vigorous strokes the picturesque and essential elements of every scene, and his flair for the eccentric, he extracted from his experiences vivid material for excellent short stories. A superficial thinker, uninterested in the analysis of character, he was not well qualified to be a novelist. Completely indifferent to all moral problems, he certainly had no interest in the soul. He is not even a highly lettered man, and by his own account has reduced his reading to a minimum. Not intellectual, but exceedingly intelligent, he drew his vast information from the spectacle of the world about him, for his special gift is that of the reporter who observes and visualizes. Instead of utilizing his cosmopolitanism to sift out all the qualities of his era, he carefully skimmed it of everything but its deformities and vices, and seems to have explored the globe with the express purpose of discovering only the worst.

Obviously mesmerized by the corruption of post-war Europe, he accepted its demoralization as irreparable. "We are inclined to believe," reads the citation from a treatise on hydrogen oxide which prefaces his *Europe galante,* "that the voluptuous sensations which many people seem recently to have experienced are due to an incipient asphyxia." This would be an appropriate introduction for most of Morand's early work. Attributing the prevailing mental and moral aberration to the purely chemical reaction from these poisonous gases, he applied himself to a. cool examination of the more colorful manifestations of the disease. If we are to take him at his word, most of his stories are personal experiences, and reveal the author now at Moscow, now at Constantinople, now at Budapest, as a roving, if usually frustrated Don Juan. Untroubled by conscience, never indulging in introspection, he writes a diary of facts and abstains from personal reflections. In addition, he possesses that rare faculty of being able to judge dispassionately a life of which he has been himself a part.

His literary bag started traveling in 1921 with *Tendres Stocks,* a collection of three short feminine portraits, which, begun as early as 1914, were later united in this single volume. The station label is London, a city which Morand knew well, since, in addition to his early years of study in England, he is said to have crossed the Channel some hundred and fifty times. The date is the World War and shortly after. The first in this triad of remarkable young women is Clarisse, the purest through whose hands the old bag has passed. She is one of those phantom creatures of whom Proust says in his preface to this book: "We adore the women of Renoir, Morand, and Giraudoux, whereas before becoming accustomed to this new and original artistry we would have refused to admit their being women at all. And we feel a desire to wander through a forest which at first sight seemed anything but a forest; let us say, a tapestry combining a thousand shades of color in which the forest shades alone were lacking." Light-hearted and irresponsible, preferring in true Giraudoux style the imitation to the genuine, cherishing knick-nacks, antiques, and old-fashioned clothes, sending clouds as gifts, cutting roses at the declaration of the War, Clarisse is the center of a little group of adoring friends, all equally young, slender, bright-eyed, and red-lipped. Behind their gaiety lurks tragedy, and a scene at Murray's Café reveals among the dancers men with arms in slings and bandaged heads, while waiters stumble over crutches.

Delphine of the second story is drawn in more somber color, for Morand now strikes that sinister note which will characterize his future work. A young French war widow who has come to London to forget her sorrows, Delphine explains: "The War of course is the cause of all my misfortunes, and at a time when the crowded hospitals resounded with strange avowals in every tongue, when the hospital trains were taken up by respectable ladies who were beside themselves at the smell of gangrene, when tea shops were opened round the Archbishopric and edges of the road were decorated with great umbrellas beneath which Annamites shielded their yellow unions, there was nothing in the city of Tours to prevent a young French 'bourgeoise' from marrying the soft-booted Russian officer who had been following her for the past two months." The convent in London where Delphine has taken lodgings must have been dangerously near the cafés, for we see her dragging her widows' weeds through the bacchanalian nightlife of the war-crazed city. With her hair unkempt and dyed tomato red, her body splotched with disease and drug injections, she has become the victim of the dissolute society in which she moves. "At first you do not know how you have become entangled in your little band of friends, but later you have the impression that it has been contrived in advance by some mysterious force. Taken to a place of amusement, you return the following day, and thus a magic ring is formed which closes in upon you, until one day, questioning every value, you totter to the brink of nothingness."

Morand next presents an ironical picture of Aurore, the back-to-nature athlete, whose only god is hygiene and who comes dangerously near falling from her pedestal of chastity. Such are the *tendres stocks,* the green shoots, of Morand's first group of women.

In *Ouvert la nuit* of the following year, he introduces six more, this time not quite so tender. Their histories, entitled "Nights," are laid in as many different countries, and each heroine embodies what Morand believes to be characteristic national traits. Presented with all the ease and variety of a rambling conversation in a drawing-room or club, these keen, sophisticated tales are alternately gay and melancholy. In a railway coach, the author's quick eye for the bizarre maneuvers a chance encounter with the loquacious, excitable Doña Remedios from Barcelona, "one of those bodies cloyed by siestas, swollen by sugar and throbbing with vows and omens: in short, a Spanish woman" (*La Nuit catalane*). A Night for the Russian Anna, of noble birth, but now reduced to serving as a waitress in a café in post-war Constantinople (*La Nuit turque*). A Night for Isabelle, a young French girl, who, living since the war in Rome and deserted by her mother, has sunk to the lowest degradation and is strangled by her mulatto lover (*La Nuit romaine*); while a no less tragic fate befalls the Jewish cabaret singer Jael, thrown into the Danube by the secret service squad when she braves the Semitic ban and returns to her native home in Budapest (*La Nuit hongroise*). A brighter note distinguishes the story of Léa, the Parisian street girl, whom the author encounters at Maxime's. Stung by the bee of constancy, she defers his advances while absorbed in the outcome of the six-day bicycle race participated in by the preferred lover, Petitmathieu. She is naturally annoyed when her new admirer becomes so fascinated by the race that he loses all interest in her (*La Nuit des six jours*). Morand's rôle of Don Juan does not dim his shrewd observation of Aïno, the Danish girl, who as the pretty secretary of a nudist society somewhere on the Baltic coast eventually has reason to brand him, its newest member, a *cochon international*.

Probably encouraged by the sensational success accorded his first series of Nights, Morand the following year brought out four more, this time masculine portraits, called *Fermé la nuit*. Continuing his custom of representing in one person the salient features of a country, he sums up Ireland in O'Patah, revolutionist and poet, sensational, nervous, vain, naïve, and sentimental; and like all poets and all Irish, adds the author, destined for the ridiculous, the tragic, and the sublime (*La Nuit de Portofino Kulm*). Pagan and sadistic Germany is exemplified by the war-impoverished Baron Egon von Strachwitz, highly cultured, blasé, puerile, and hysterical, who raises poisonous reptiles and carries courtesy so far as to lend his wife to a visiting author (*La Nuit de Charlottenburg*). The harassed and over-worked French minister is equally true to his race in rebounding after every setback (*La Nuit de Babylone*); while "the hideous victory of the Levantine over the Occident" may be seen in the cruel picture of the Armenian Jew and beauty doctor Habib, and the world of middle-aged London society women who submit to the most humiliating beauty treatments at his hands. This intelligent and cold-blooded Easterner uses their vanity to win from their politically influential husbands favorable inter-cession for the Armenians (*La Nuit de Putney*).

The following year, in 1924, Morand produced his first, rather abbreviated novel, *Lewis et Irène*. If we follow the career of this young millionaire banker, natural son of a Belgian finan-cier and an unknown French mother, we visit the rather dubious salon of Mme Magnac with whom Lewis shares in common a taste for "gluttony, expenditure, and women"; we read his note-book containing the names of the 413 women he has possessed during two years after the Armistice; swim with him in the Mediterranean, where clinging to a fishing boat, he sees for the first time the self-reliant, healthy-bodied Irène, a young widow of English-Greek extraction and directress of the Bank Apostolatus at Trieste. After an elliptical courtship, conducted mainly by telegrams, they marry and spend their honeymoon at Irène's old home in Greece. Soon haunted by nostalgic dreams of Paris, the young bridegroom leads Irène back to France, where they eventually resume their respective professional ca-reers. If Lewis is jealous of his wife's superior business ability, she on her side never forgives him for his waning love, and so they part, never to meet again. However, they maintain the most amicable business relations and, regardless of the strain on the reader's credulity, write to each other every day.

If, in America, woman's part in business has long been regarded as a commonplace, in France this miracle was accomplished at a much later date and after a harder struggle. In fact, to the Frenchman such a usurping of man's prerogative was looked upon as nothing less than an outrage. Hence the importance of the social issue involved in Morand's novel. In contrasting Irène's perseverance, prudence, and reliability with Lewis' capriciousness, extravagance, lack of balance and logic, Morand is plainly championing the woman, just as he does in a later novel, *Champions du monde,* where four American college students set out in 1909 to conquer the world, but are forced to concede the victory twenty years later to four women.

After the completion of *Lewis et Irène,* Morand's bag started out on more extensive journeys. It was whisked through several continents, and Morand writes a book about each one. The *Chroniques* and *Voyages,* the general title selected for these books, mark a turning-point in his career. Having gradually become more interested in the souls of races rather than of individuals, in this new series of books Morand swerves to sociology and ethnology. To gather his material, he "cycled along the latitudes" and "coasted down the longitudes"; he "toyed with the center of the earth"; he "united the equatorial sash." A world tour beginning with the United States and extending through Japan, China, and India resulted in *Rien que la terre.* A dip into Africa gave *Paris-Tombouctou.* A few months in South America furnished material for *L'Air indien.* Another visit to the United States brought forth *Champions du monde.* He lingered long enough in individual cities to write *New-York* and *Londres;* long enough on a bygone epoch to write a book called *1900.* One French critic attributes to him a dressmaker's flair for anticipating the coming vogue. Morand was on hand with *Bouddha vivant* at the very moment when Europeans were beginning to languish for an Asiatic cult. He was equally in fashion with Irène, the unsentimental modern business woman.

Coincident with the invasion of Paris by negroes and jazz, he wrote *Magie noire*. His *1900* appeared just as his countrymen were beginning to turn backward to this neglected period. Since Morand has recently published two new books, *Rococo,* whose chief story deals with ballet girls, and *France-la-Doulce,* which satirizes certain abuses in the cinematographic world, it may be assumed that Europe is about to undergo a revival of interest in choreography and the film. For Morand, sometimes called the "planetary chronicler," is the barometer of the hour.

If he says that his bag is discolored by sea water and sweat, this must be taken figuratively, since Morand is a traveler *de luxe*. His real baggage must be a very elegant affair whose only wear and tear is that involved in Pullmans, yachts, and airplanes, a conspicuous item of his equipment being the cheque-book hung about his neck. Like Barnabooth, his counterpart in fiction, when Morand sets out upon a journey, he demands speed and comfort. "Thanks to the airplane," he informs us in *Paris-Tombouctou,* "our generation has recovered some of the time lost in the days of horses and schooners." When he says that the modern world "constructs locomotives which go more swiftly than its ideas," he formulates the very reproach often addressed to him. In his hastily compiled travelogues, in which like "a bullet in flight" he jots down his fleeting impressions, he has perforce glanced so superficially at all these passing land-scapes that he has pierced no deeper than their external physical aspect. He ends by finding his planet astonishingly small. "Often, when I am walking in the neighborhood of the Opéra in Paris, I say to myself: 'London is at the end of the rue Lafayette; to go to Madrid I have only to descend three steps and it is just in front of me.'" "What! Nothing but the earth?" is his famous cry. "Only this tiny world which we shall soon be able to tour for eighty francs? No violet, pink, or green races to add to the spots of yellow, black, and white? No new *Mayflower* to hop

off at dawn for Saturn? Our fathers were sedentary. Our sons
will be even more so, for they will have no place but this earth
to move about in."

He notes that races have intermingled without either understanding or sympathy. "The vice which characterizes the years
1920–1930 is indifference," he writes in *Bouddha vivant.* "Our
best books from Gide to Proust are manuals of indifference. The
husbands who abduct for their own purposes the lovers of their
wives; the countries who strangle each other after having been
allies; the generals—enemies only yesterday—who now dine together; the assassinations which amuse the world: all this is not
madness, softness, or perversity; it is indifference"—or else
hatred, which Morand thinks grows in direct proportion to the
number of passports visaed. "Take France and England, for
example. These two nations, among the greatest of the world,
are separated by only forty-five minutes of sea. But despite more
than ten centuries of intercourse, they are as far apart as Persia
and the Antilles. They have shed blood in the same cause, yet, if
we set aside their official declarations of love, they live in mutual
ignorance and contempt. It is only hypocrisy that prevents us
from calling foreigners swine and unclean, as the Orientals do.
And as for the Orient, who would have thought of seeking it
while it possessed a wisdom and a secret of life now lost? Why
do we become interested only at the moment when it is sinking
into the quicksand of fanatic nationalism, succumbing to the
gluttony of gold and the new needs created by the fertile absurdity of Western trade? And since it is not mutual riches,
but mutual poverty that nations exchange, might not the stupidity of reciprocal ignorance be preferable to the reciprocal hatred
of familiarity?"

However, Morand's own treatment of America is not no-
ticeably tolerant. Analyzing the United States, as he does in
Champions du monde, he betrays irritation at foreign points of

view opposed to his own. He shows the natural annoyance of a Frenchman at the crude and tyrannic rule of women in America. "What mightn't the Americans do if they weren't married! America in the early days was the country of men, and from it emerged a very small number of sublime women. The sexes in that America were separated in country churches. Nowadays there are too many women; American politics show every flaw which history attributes to petticoat rule: capriciousness, bursts of anger, sentimental thrills, extravagant spending—not to mention industry, that marriage with matter; and commerce, that prostitution; and overproduction, that excess of amorous zeal. Europe has the muscles and members of a man, but America is a woman—a woman fond of soldiers, boxers, youth, tenors, evangelical preachers, ecstasies, silk, and kisses on the lips." Like the average European, he cannot comprehend the American naïveté which attempts to reconcile financial interests with high-sounding ethics, purity of ideals with monetary returns. Neither can he understand the state's intervention in matters of private life; that, he feels, is the business of religion. "America, full of selfishness outside, and of generosity within, Puritan at heart, Slavic in its senses, Greek in its muscles—a land that I admire for its ostrich-like stomach, absorbing everything and restoring nothing—an America that remains uncreative in spite of her vast output: she at least is perfectly happy. But for how long?" It must be admitted that some of Morand's strictures on America have the unpleasant sting of truth. A keener diagnostician, however, would not mistake activity for contentment, and would recognize that far from being happy, the Americans are a sad people. If, to judge from *Champions du monde,* he has only seen in America a country of Y.M.C.A.'s, prize fights, beauty contests, and women who call their husbands "baby," he has merely skimmed the surface.

Whatever gadfly of the spirit drives Morand from one end

of the world to the other, he admits that it is not travel but movement that he loves, and that a complete sense of well-being comes only in the moment of displacement. "My one fixed point," he says, "is this idea of change, and I shall never be ashamed of my life so long as it continues to possess mobility. As far back as I can remember there existed in me a desire to be elsewhere, an implacable desire as tenacious as a wound." Perhaps it was a wound that induced this insatiable globe-trotter to choose a Medusa for his crest: "Mobile, the Medusa dreams of rest; inert, she dreams of movement." Thus Morand complains of the French who greet travel with reluctance and procrastination. "Are my countrymen, then, so happy," he asks, "that commotion means only the worst that fate has in store for them?" Perhaps this should read: Is Morand, then, so unhappy that commotion means the best that fate has to offer? One critic has found a name for the literary geography of recent years: "itineraries of flight." In Morand's nomadism it is not hard to detect an instinct for evasion. If, in his later books, he seeks a diversity of races and climates, it is probably to escape the thought of something worse—the depressing failure of occidental civilization. At all events, in one of his recent articles, he cries out: "Air, I pray, air!" which might be interpreted as meaning that, having discovered the world to be in a state of putrefaction and decay, having lifted the lid off this ignominious mess, Morand is suffering a belated attack of virtue. Comparing Morand to "a gentleman with a bad hangover who curses his existence and dreams of clear waters, blue skies, and green pastures," one critic suggests that the author of *L'Europe galante* might begin to purify the atmosphere by burning his own books.

His early stories were so successful not only because he focused his camera on unusual scenes and faces, but because of the highly individual retouching he gave to every snapshot. As an attaché in the Paris Foreign Office under Giraudoux where they directed propaganda for French letters, Morand doubtless profited from his association with this master imagist. One critic, Lucien Dubech, delights in ridiculing both of them: "If I had received from heaven the art of comedy, I should like to imagine a dialogue between these two honorable diplomats. In their ordinary conversation do they employ those famous new relationships which so impress the literary snobs? If one of them speaks *à la Giraudoux* and the other replies *à la Morand,* the effect must be astonishing." However, most people enjoy these "new relationships," and are glad that Morand caught from the flippant and irrepressible Giraudoux the knack of creating ladies resembling bonbons; eyes opening like fried eggs; faces suggesting department stores; and villas twisted like marshmallows. They like the freshness of vision which makes Morand's dancing couples "turn round an imaginary axis and twist out the waltz like a dishcloth from which melody streams"; the droll humor which causes the Grand Duchess "although naturally extinguished, to light up at the approach of a man and shine like a candle." It is refreshing to hear that Louisa, because of the languid movement of her eyes, suggests an early bringing-up on a railway line where only slow trains passed; that Léa, putting on her evening wrap, envelopes herself in ninety-eight white rabbits; that the Germans made war on England because they believed British tailors had cut their clothes badly on purpose; that Frenchmen's faces are like drawing-rooms with too much in them—moustaches, a beard, spectacles, warts, and beauty spots covered with down; that Clarisse "right from her shoulders was divided instantly into two legs, thin and pointed in the form of a compass, advancing and pricking the pavement."

At his best, Morand is capable of such passages as: "It is night; a clear night, isolated in a rainy spring whose warm blue humidity it continues to exhale. The windows are open; we, with our elbows on the balcony. You lean over to breathe the scent of the fresh-cut grass which rises from Kensington and mingles with the animal perfume of the dance. The acid green of your Longhi cloak is a curve on the vivid orange of a Japanese bridge curved like an ass's back; the masks squeeze against the parapet a woman with bared bosom who laughs as she throws bread to the carp. While the Venetian *bauta* gives your face a setting of shadow letting only a strange mouth be seen, a mouth of chemical red, the night girdles the whole feast with a rich, velvety shade, with no light save that of Charles's Wain with its inverted wheels, falling on us in a motionless vertical tumble." This scene is followed immediately by another, even more successful, of daytime in the country. "The tennis court seems to have been cut in the truncated crown of this hill whence the country, like a pompous and futile park, undulates gently to the sea. Picking up his gestures and his shadow round himself, a young man clad in white duck accompanies with an elongated gesture the ball which he serves to his awaiting adversary. On a knoll of blue grass, some young women in cherry, yellow, green, cherry jumpers gather round the tea, served on a rattan table. And the center of all this light, this glistening joy, the luminous axle of this circle of women, framed by the still vaster wheel of field and sky, is the silver teapot which sings like wasps on a tart: its reflecting lid sends back a convex image of the sky, the shadow of the trees; its ribbed body, the thinned lines of the faces, and in narrow streaks, the jumpers, cherry, yellow, green, cherry."

Countless examples attest to his skill in vivid imagery. "Under the weight of the railroad bridge and packages of newspapers, Fleet Street folds, collapses, then, as if under the thrust of a springboard, remounts towards Saint Paul's, climbs over it, and leaps to the sky of copper-colored pink." Frequently he presents richly embroidered enumerations without a verb, expanding at times to entire pages. His elliptical style, like his speed in traveling, is sharply symptomatic of the rush and agitation of modern times. Possessing an inexhaustible vocabulary, he can talk in the sporting lingo of the velodrome, or switch glibly to the technicalities of finance. To acquire this last for *Lewis et Irène,* he is said to have spent three months in a banking house.

Précieux and heavily ornate, at times Morand is not easy to read. Even Proust, that past master of involved sentence structure, found him arduous, for he says: "Morand is generally rather tiring and difficult to understand because he brings together things never before associated. We follow him quite well until halfway through the sentence, and there our attention flags. And we feel that it is only because this new writer is a nimbler fellow than we." This criticism, indeed, might apply to Morand's master, Giraudoux himself. However, with the exception of *Tendres Stocks,* there is little in Morand's brutality of vision to suggest the delicate discrimination and wit which characterize Giraudoux. Not that Morand is lacking in a certain catchy humor. "Is she a woman of letters?" asks one of his characters; to which the answer is: "No, I think she's chaste."

Where Giraudoux's universe is like a still landscape bathed in sunshine, Morand's much more vigorous art presents a realistic world with sharp architectural lines and intense shadows. Far from ignoring ugliness, Morand welcomes and emphasizes it, for he believes that by coarsening and depoetizing he avoids the commonplace. When his picture needs a cat, he may be depended on to select one that limps. If a theatre is full of people, he focuses the spotlight on those feminine backs with "ossicles and knotty bands, itching and flat like paving stones." Granted that Barcelona lacks beauty, Morand presses the point by comparing its porters' lodges to tumors, its chimneys to varicose veins.

However, it might be a mistake to suggest the removal of

these ugly realities, for when in his later books he resorts less frequently to imagery, freaks of style, and brutal fancies, how dull and tame he becomes! Grown used to these verbal cocktails, we find insipid a less highly flavored drink. Expanding his vision in the *Chroniques* and the *Voyages,* Morand devotes less attention to his style, and his literary distinction proceeds in inverse ratio to this expansion. He states somewhere that, weary of his former pyrotechnics, which everyone was imitating, he strove to sober and simplify his phrase. Whether or not Morand has ceased to value sophisticated recognition, he has been content for a number of years to produce a series of none too carefully written best-sellers. He evidently prefers to be read once by the profitable multitude than to be reread by the discriminating few. His *New-York* has had 264 editions; *Tendres Stocks,* but twenty-one. If formerly he wrote because he traveled, he now travels because he wants to write. Where, in *Tendres Stocks,* you could imagine yourself turning the fanciful if artificial pages of Giraudoux, in *Magie noire* or *Champions du monde* you might be perusing a *Harper's Bazaar,* while much of his travel literature is hardly more than glorified Baedeker. Stepping into immediate fame with *Tendres Stocks,* creating a literary furor with *Ouvert la nuit,* adding to his triumphs with *Fermé la nuit,* Morand never surpassed nor equaled his early efforts. Indeed, it would have been difficult to improve upon his first masterpieces. There were many gifts he lacked; those he did possess were preëminent. A mature and skilful artist from the first, he dazzled the world by the audacity of his imagery, the keenness of his observation, his glitter, originality, and verve. His very vitality proved a pitfall, for in addition to his diplomatic duties and his travels to the four corners of the globe, he likes to keep his name before the public with one book, sometimes two, a year, and it is not to be expected that five novels, six collections of short stories, seven volumes of travels, one pseudo-historical study, countless magazine articles, and, to omit nothing, the inevitable volumes of adolescent verse—all of these appearing within the short span of some thirteen years—could maintain an equal standard of excellence. It is more surprising that his talent was born as it were full grown, than that with time its original brilliance tarnished.

Colette

Women geniuses are still conspicuously rare. Madame Colette is rare from every point of view. A distinguished artist and a fascinating personality, she has added a picturesque splash of color to the patchwork of contemporary French letters. Here is an author who, in an age obsessed by war and social unrest, forgets that there is anything in life but love. Even in a woman such indifference to the problems of the outside world is noticeable. When reproached by a friend for writing books which deal only with love, Colette muses: "If this man, who was handsome and charming, had not himself been hurrying to a rendezvous at that moment, perhaps he could have told me what is worthy, either in a novel or outside one, to take the place of love." It is sometimes assumed that writers who ignore the domain of the intellect are themselves deficient in it. Commenting on the fact that Loti had been elected to the French Academy, Anatole France remarked: "The only one among us who has genius, has no brains." If Colette ignores the mind to concentrate on the heart and senses, it does not mean any less work for her acute intelligence.

Distinctly feminine in her predilection for sentimental reminiscence, Colette is almost exclusively inspired by her own emotional experiences. In true Narcissus fashion, she hovers entranced before a mirror. There she sees much she dare not disclose, yet what she can reveal must have an air of candor. Autobiographical writers may confess more than the world wants to hear; or through their omissions they may create false impressions. André Gide takes a gambler's chance and with *Si le grain ne meurt* tells all; Colette, telling only the partial truth, strives to create a legend about her name. It is a very pretty legend, and many will prefer it to the truth. If Colette had not chosen to weave her life so closely with her art, her readers might feel it unjustifiable to pry into withheld recesses. Faced with the discrepanices between what she says and what she thinks of love, one must seek the real Colette through certain unwitting betrayals.

Born far from Paris in Saint-Sauveur on the borderline between Burgundy and Nivernais, Colette romped through her childhood in pagan innocence. Her name was Sidonie-Gabrielle Colette, but she was better known by nicknames, "Minet-Chéri," "Bel-Gazou." Adoring her family, her old home, animals and all forms of nature, she lived in an atmosphere of love. If Colette had never written another word, she would still be famous for *La Maison de Claudine,* which is devoted to her childhood. In evocatory pages unsurpassed by Anatole France or Alphonse Daudet, she presents her father, a retired army officer with a wooden leg but a soft heart, who scandalizes an old lady of the community by offering to initiate her into the delights of love for forty sous and a package of tobacco; her brother, who at the age of thirteen had a passion for graveyards and built miniature cemeteries in the garden; her mischievous schoolmates chewing blotting paper; the timeworn benches in the village school, constructed apparently to make hunchbacks of the children; and her cat Fanchette with its attack of dysentery.

But it is to her mother that Colette's pen returns most often in affectionate retrospect. "I am the daughter of a woman," she writes in *La Naissance du jour,* "who in a little disgraceful community, miserly and restricted, opened her village home to wandering dogs, tramps, and pregnant servant girls. I am the daughter of a woman who in constant despair of finding money for the needy, would run through the snow and wind to cry at the houses of the rich that a child had just been born beside some destitute hearth and needed swaddling clothes. How could I forget that I was born of a woman who, trembling, would lower her dazzled, wrinkled face among the prickles of some cactus plant which gave signs of flowering, a woman who never ceased to bloom herself throughout three-quarters of a century." Thanks to Colette's verve and wit, we see this "mother-dog"—the word is her own—in breathless search of her scattered offspring: "The children, where are, where can they be?" Let one of them get married, the anxious mother is ever fearful for her puppy. "What! Am I always to worry about these children! There is my eldest daughter, for example, who has gone off with that gentleman." "What do you mean, gone off?" her husband asks. "Well, she married him, didn't she?" the mother replies; "Married or not married, she has gone off just the same with a gentleman she hardly knew." And looking at her husband with tender suspiciousness, she adds: "For after all, what are you to me? You aren't even related." Other glimpses of Colette's mother reveal her making mittens for real puppies, foregoing a trip in order to see her cactus bloom, cherishing a wounded but destructive caterpillar, protecting the spider which spins its web above her bed and descends nightly into her bowl of chocolate. It is tempting to dwell on the features of this extraordinary and delightful woman, not only because as one of the principal figures in *La Maison de Claudine, La Naissance du jour,* and *Sido* (her mother's nickname), she was the inspiration for some of Colette's finest work, but because the daughter inherited many of her mother's engaging traits. To the maternal strain in her blood Colette owes her domestic instincts, her love of everything that grows and lives, her spirit of independence and her warm charity. Doubtless, even in the shaping of her sex life, Colette's mother-complex played its part.

Her education—aside from the long hours spent in her father's library and the longer hours spent outdoors—was confined to the communal school in Saint-Sauveur. Except for a brief trip to Brussels as a child of six, and a two-weeks' stay in Paris in her sixteenth year, she had remained almost entirely in her native village. What she had seen of city life had filled her with aversion, and all she brought back were memories of "cubes of houses without gardens, where no cat mewed behind the dining-room door, no dog stretched carpet-like before the fireplace to be trod upon, and where the hand in search of some cordial caress only knocked against cold marble, wood, and inanimate velvets," all of which she left with "starved senses and suffering the urgent need to touch some living fleece, warm feathers, and moist flowers."

Soon she had to leave these early haunts, for in her twentieth year she married Henry Gauthier-Villars, and went to live in Paris. Whatever may have been her later reactions to this husband, who was some fourteen years her senior, in her early married life at least, he fascinated her. An inveterate man-about-town and pleasure-seeker, he dragged his young bride, untamed and startled fledgling that she was, through a mad round of parties, and introduced her to all the salons, night clubs, and bohemian circles of Paris.

If Colette never conformed to her husband's conception of a thorough woman of the world, but only complained of headaches as a result of their nightly dissipations, she was none the less to prove useful. Gauthier-Villars, who under the pseudonyms of "Maugis" and "Willy" was an art critic and a writer of some note, foresaw the commercial value of his wife's naïve and charming memories. He made the shrewd proposition that they become literary collaborators and write about her early life. This

was the origin of *Claudine à l'école,* which appeared in 1900.
This first book met with such instantaneous success that Colette
and Willy wrote three more in the same vein (*Claudine à
Paris,* 1901; *Claudine en ménage,* 1902; and *Claudine s'en va,*
1903). If Willy reaped the glory, these novels being signed by
his name only, Colette wrote the books, for her husband's chief
contributions were anecdotes and puns. Indulgent critics bestow
all Claudine's desirable qualities on Colette, leaving the objec-
tionable traits to her fictitious heroine, who was a young girl
raised in exactly the same milieu as Colette and endowed with
similar tastes. Like her creator, Claudine goes to Paris, is home-
sick for the country, and marries an older man who, besides being openly unfaithful to her, corrupts her by thrusting her into
the arms of another woman. If Claudine is lonely and abandoned at a period when Colette was still living with her husband; if Annie, usually considered Colette's prototype, divorces
the unfaithful Alain (*Claudine s'en va*), the Claudine stories
are sometimes autobiographical by anticipation, for it is characteristic of Colette first to conceive in a book what later she is
actually to experience.

After her divorce in 1906, Colette found herself at the mercy
of an unfriendly world. The Claudine books, daringly flavored
as they were with sexual perversion, had created scandal; her
divorce had not improved her reputation; and the friends she had
acquired through Willy sided with her husband. Perfumes, ice
creams, neckwear, lotions, and cigarettes flourished under the
trade-mark "Claudine," but the real Claudine was destitute and
obliged to seek her living on the stage. Although she danced
nightly in pantomimes and music-hall reviews, Colette had no
intention of abandoning her literary career. Scribbling in her
leisure moments, she first completed a novel begun before the
separation from her husband. That is why in *La Retraite sentimentale* (1907) Claudine makes as it were her posthumous

appearance. This time she is represented as a tender, faithful wife, sequestered in the country, where she is awaiting the return of Renaud, who is ill in Switzerland. Although the memory of her erotic aberrations with another woman is still "a strange little serpent not yet entirely dead," the heroine prefers to believe herself a "one-man" woman, who, having given herself once and for all in a single love, is fated to terminate her days in solitude. Aside from what is purely imaginary in this story, the real Colette is easily recognizable in the Claudine who moves light-heartedly among her bees, toads, and flowers, and who, when the husband dies, is lured back to life and hope. The same philosophy is expressed in her next book, *Les Vrilles de la vigne* (1908), a series of short autobiographical sketches. In one of these, seeking to console a friend who has been abandoned by her husband, the author exclaims: "Oh you, like me, won't die from this. You will experience irregular, capricious truces in your suffering, but you have something worse in store. A moment will come when you will have almost completely ceased to suffer, and it is then that you will become a real soul in pain, wandering and seeking you know not what and what you fear to know."

With *La Vagabonde* (1910), four years have passed since Colette's divorce, and she now realizes more fully what it means to be defenseless and alone. She has changed her heroine's name to Renée, but in this thirty-four year old divorcée, whom a disastrous marriage has driven to a mediocre living on the stage, Colette speaks out more boldly in the first person than ever before. She has succeeded in thrusting Taillandy (alias Willy) from her heart; yet she cannot forget the injuries he inflicted, and her smoldering resentment flares up with unexpected fury. Her three years of squalor as a music-hall artist, with meals snatched in stations, nights passed in second-rate hotels and sleeping-cars, were experiences which intensified her wrath against her husband, whose memory she now evokes as "a paternal lover seasoning his brief infatuation for her with incestuous trimmings," "a worn-out, disillusioned artist adorning his waning autumn with a delicate idyl," "an inveterate libertine and seducer," "a brutal and cowardly business man." "And what remains of my life after these eight years of marriage and three of separation?" asks the resentful Renée. "Something resembling one of those puzzles of 250 irregular and multicolored pieces of wood. Must I fit together piece by piece the early setting? Alas! someone has jumbled together all the lines of that sweet scene, and I should no longer find even the ruined remains of the blue roof embroidered with yellow lichens, nor the Virginia creeper and the deep, birdless forest." "But if you now live alone," a friend reminds her, "it is because you wish it so." "Yes, certainly I wish it. But there are days when solitude for a woman of my age is like a strong wine which intoxicates you with liberty, other days when it is a bitter tonic, still others when it is a poison which makes you beat your head against the wall." By stressing her heroine's early hours of wistful solitude, Colette renders the opportunity all the more tempting when a new love invades her life. World-weary, she has almost decided to marry the rich and worthy Maxime, when the ludicrous image of a life with this conventional, humdrum husband intervenes. Rather than be dominated by a master and bound to a narrow, pompous existence, she chooses to remain the lonely vagabond. "In spite of my first marriage and this second romance, I shall always be a sort of old maid so much in love with Love that no love seems sufficiently beautiful."

L'Entrave (1913), a sequel to *La Vagabonde,* shows Renée at Nice some three years later, and financially independent through an inheritance. Still skeptical of love, but suffering from loneliness, she finally consents to a liaison with a young man named Jean, imposing the condition, however, that this shall remain an unsentimental physical union. After reluctantly adapting herself to her lover's moods, but relying on his frequent absences to indulge her taste for freedom, she is astonished to discover that she has gradually fallen in love with him. "I measured the full extent of the danger I was running the day I began to scorn what you were giving me. The moment I realized what you were not giving me, I entered within that cold shadow which leads one straight towards love." While Jean, soon sa-tiated, and seeking some loophole of escape from their love, says: "I am afraid that we two are no longer sufficiently in need of one another," Renée cries: "He is more necessary to me than air and water, and I prefer him to those fragile possessions which a woman names her dignity and self-esteem." By exerting all her intelligence and ingenuity, she wins her lover back, although she resents the price she pays for this victory—her freedom. "My place has been usurped by Jean, who has become the eager vagabond, while I look on in shackles."

After *L'Envers du Music-hall* (1913) with its account of Colette's experiences on the stage; after *Les Heures longues* (1917), which reveals her as a war nurse; after *La Femme cachée* (1924), which foreshadows her divorce two years later from her second husband, Henry de Jouvenel; after *La Maison de Claudine* (1923), in which the author definitely identifies herself with Claudine in speaking of her childhood; in 1928 the curtain falls on the Claudine-Renée-Colette drama with *La Naissance du jour*. This final chapter in a life drawing to its close recounts an aging woman's farewell to love. The tragedy of this renunciation lies not so much in the difference of ages between Colette, who is now past fifty, and her young admirer, as in her realization of that moment in her life when she can gaze upon his virile beauty without a tremor of desire. For the first time in thirty years, she is confronted with the fact that love is no longer the guiding motive in her life, and her cry of

"Oh God! grant that he be here!" is now altered to "Oh God! grant that he may not be here!" This death of love is not treated as tragedy but rather as a liberation. Colette had hitherto been obliged to worship two gods; she can now reserve herself exclusively for Pan.

If the autobiographical novels are Colette's official confessions, her works of impersonal fiction contain the lamentations of other suffering women, all victims like herself of man's cruelty. Having so long scrutinized her own soul, she now feels sufficient confidence in her powers to probe the souls of others, but in turning from the full-face image, she has only adjusted the mirror to give side views and oblique reflections. Her great series of creative novels begins in 1917 with *Mitsou*, and includes *Chéri* (1920); its sequel, *La Fin de Chéri* (1925); *Le Blé en herbe* (1923); *La Seconde* (1929); and *Duo* (1934). These books, the fruit of her maturity, constitute her finest work. If up to this time she modeled charming statuettes in clay, in the *Chéri* books and *La Seconde* she proves her ability to carve in rock. Minne in *L'Ingénue libertine* is more phantom than woman in her attempts to solve the mysteries of sex; *Mitsou* is pure fancy with its story of a naïve and obscure music-hall actress, whose unsuspected capacity for emotion is awakened through her love for an army officer on leave; while the fifteen-year-old quasi-maternal Vinca in *Le Blé en herbe* is just as shadowy when, in this modern version of Daphnis and Chloe, she heroically offers her body to her youthful and despondent lover. All of these tales are moving, even poignant, but it is not until *Chéri* that Colette establishes her reputation as a creative genius.

Rumor has it that even *Chéri*, this story of the passion of an aging courtesan and her young gigolo, is only disguised autobiography. The illegitimate son of an enriched cocotte, Chéri has grown into a vain, soft, pampered youth of seventeen, who is redeemed from total mediocrity only by his great physical beauty and compelling charm. Among his mother's friends moves Léa, also a demi-mondaine, who is living on the fortune she has amassed, but who, unlike his mother, is still seductive in spite of the fact that she is over fifty. A kiss from Chéri suddenly rouses the passion of this woman whose interest in him has hitherto been maternal. Their liaison lasts seven years until that day when Léa, confronted with the inexorable specter of old age, is obliged to relinquish Chéri in marriage to a rich young girl. But if Léa abdicates with dignity before this, her final and greatest passion, Chéri's case is not so simple. Barely returned from his honeymoon, he is haunted by memories of his former mistress plus the realization that she is the only woman he can ever love. As if the earlier chapters were only a prelude to one last colossal scene, Colette in some twenty pages of almost epic grandeur describes the reunion of the lovers with such unerring instinct that the reader forgets the narrator's consummate art to follow hypnotized every word or movement of the protagonists. Léa's hopes of holding Chéri are quickly shattered, and after a single night together an old and haggard woman stands behind a parted blind to gaze upon her retreating lover, who upon emerging the next morning into the sunny street, raises his head towards the sky and flowering chestnut trees and inflates his lungs with air, as though escaping from a prison.

Léa and Chéri are destined to meet once again. In *La Fin de Chéri* we learn that seven years have passed and that the War has intervened. Léa is now over sixty, while Chéri is in his early thirties. Their history is a tragedy of figures, and Colette's art is to prevent this from degenerating into a farce. If Chéri has never returned to Léa, he has become a completely benumbed young man with no thought for other women. A chance mention of her name revives his dormant passion and he goes to see her. "A woman was seated writing before a desk.

Chéri distinguished a broad back, and a bulging goose-fleshed neck, above which sturdy gray hair emerged in the manner of his mother's. "Well, Léa is not alone. Who is that old lady there?" But the old woman was Léa, and in representing Chéri as failing to recognize his former mistress, Colette evokes in one stroke the ravages of "devouring time." Léa, finished with sex and coquetry, has settled down to the comfortable tranquillity of old age. Chéri, without further motive for existence, finds his sole nourishment in the memories of a vanished love; making a fetish of this phantom Léa, he hires one of her old friends to talk of her and show him photographs. Finally this last resource is exhausted, and one day, lying down among the pictures, he murmurs: "Léa, darling," and calmly presses a revolver to his head.

La Seconde, ranking with *Chéri* as one of Colette's master-pieces, is the history of Fanny Farou, who still loves her husband, a playwright, although she knows him to be unfaithful. Discovering little by little the jealous torments of Jane, her husband's secretary and mistress, who shares their home and his inconstancy, the wife remains silent through dignity and pity for the other woman. When circumstances force Fanny and Jane to an explanation, Farou, who enters unexpectedly, is asked to choose between them. Lacking courage in face of this dilemma—for he wishes to keep his wife and change his mistresses—he leaves the decision to the women. When he returns home a few hours later and finds them still in council, he stealthily tiptoes away from the door he dares not open. The women, left face to face, feel only contempt for this man, who is the weakest of the three. Impelled by the necessity of maintaining domestic peace, and fortified by their mutual understanding, they unite their forces against a common enemy. "You, Fanny, are much better as a woman than Farou is as a man, much, much better."

In *Duo,* a woman has deceived her husband, who discovers her act a year later when to her it has become a faint and indifferent memory. To the wife the offense seems inconsequential, and she cannot understand Michel's grotesque and tragic reactions. Only at his suicide, after an ineffectual eight-day struggle with his jealousy, does she realize the extent of the wound she has inflicted.

The examination of these novels, cursory though it has been, reveals a unifying theme. If we discount the early *Claudine* books as being written under Willy's supervision, there remain some ten books which deal with love between men and women. When this gallery of portraits is passed in review, it is striking to discover not one flattering picture of a man. There is Maxime, whom Renée's desertion has rendered more ridiculous than pathetic; there is the lieutenant in *Mitsou,* overshadowed by a plebeian little actress, who, if her grammar is poorer, has the warmer heart; there is the weak and whining Phil in *Le Blé en herbe,* sinking into insignificance by the side of the valiant little Vinca; there is Chéri, too cowardly to live, while the stoic Léa "carries on"; there is the polygamous Farou, content to tiptoe out of danger; and there is finally, in *Duo,* the crushed and jealous Michel, whom Colette almost seems to mock in his despair. With the exception of Chéri, one of the most vivid of all her characters, these masculine figures are easily effaced, leaving only a vague and slightly disagreeable memory. Always faintly sarcastic and contemptuous when she speaks of men, Colette never fails to endow them with beautiful bodies. She excels in sensuous descriptions of nude or scantily covered men, especially when these are young and sunburnt. Her scorn is reserved for their moral defects.

It is over her heroines that her heart expands. Her natural enthusiasm is for woman, to whom she invariably attributes the better judgment, the warmer imagination, the keener perception, the more intense feeling, and the greater self-control. Let a man deceive a woman in a Colette book, he is sure to be a monster of cruelty and ingratitude, she a dignified and suffering martyr. When the woman is the transgressor, this sympathy for the victim is replaced by prompt derision. While her heroines never neglect a chance to protest their undying love for some one man, under these lyric protestations there is a cool appraisal or some witty barb at their expense. When Fanny contemplates her sleeping husband, all that she discovers in his face is "an ingenuousness full of its own importance." When he meets with success in his literary career and is flattered by admiring women, she remarks: "Why yes, he has written another play. But if he were a woodcarver, or had invented an electric brush or a new fly-swatter, would they be leaning over him thus as if he were the Nativity?" Colette's heroines are never lacking in physical desire; indeed, this is what makes them slaves to man. Annie, in *La Retraite sentimentale,* though a nymphomaniac, is typical in one respect of all of them, for, deprived of men, she says: "It is not grief from which I suffer, but from a sense of something lacking, an amputation, a physical uneasiness so hard to define that I confuse it with hunger, thirst, headache or fatigue." Nevertheless Colette's heroines despise these in-struments of their pleasure, for her psychology attributes to women what is usually considered a purely masculine trait.

But man, the necessity, is at the same time the woman's enemy, who "kills the thing he loves." Her heroines give their bodies, but withhold their souls, for they find all fusion with the masculine mind impossible. In *L'Entrave* and *Chéri,* Colette provides examples, it is true, of women who give both soul and body, but Renée begrudges her self-renunciation, while with Léa, the courtesan, there was not much mind to surrender, the chief regret of this inarticulate woman being that her lover made her house untidy. The only male characters receiving sympathetic treatment at Colette's hands are Chéri who, nursed, coddled, fashioned, and absorbed by an older woman, is more a plaything than a man; and Alain, the hero of *La Chatte,* likewise endowed with feminine traits and charms. On the other hand, the one woman in Colette's books who obviously irritates her is Alain's wife Camille, for she, with her decided, brutal, insistent nature, is masculine in type. Colette is too much of a feminist not to resent woman's subordinate position, and most of her heroines are invested with her own hostility towards man.

It is difficult to decide how far Colette's attitude is biased by her first matrimonial experience, possessing as we do only her version of the story. In spite of Colette's constant reminders that she never recovered from her first great disillusionment in love, one might assume that she did find other, if feminine, consolations. We have only to recall the occasion when she was hissed off the stage in what has been called "the scandal of the Moulin Rouge." She endeavors to prove that because of the wounds inflicted by man, two women are often thrown upon each other for solace and mutual protection. "Maxime could never understand my earlier experiences," says Renée in *La Vagabonde.* "For him, two women, clasped in each other's arms, would only remain a lewd couple and not represent, as they should, the melancholy and touching spectacle of two weak creatures who have perhaps taken refuge in each other to weep and sleep, to flee from the cruelty of man, and to taste, rather than any pleasure, the bitter happiness of feeling themselves alike, degraded and forgotten." This explanation does not altogether coincide with Colette's statement that "women and girls can receive masculine compliments on their sexual attraction without flinching, but that the same praise from another woman is more disturbing and gives more satisfying pleasure"; nor with her sympathetic attitude in *Ces Plaisirs* (1932), towards various forms of abnormal sexuality.

Since Colette cannot help creating characters in her own image, her heroines naturally reflect her own peculiar outlook, but she is feminine and illogical enough to disclaim all such resemblances. When she hears that her books give the impression that she herself scorns love, she exclaims with irritation: "It is impossible to conceal the jealous discouragement and hostility which takes possession of me when I learn that people insist on seeing my own portrait in my novels." And yet, a short time earlier in *La Naissance du jour,* Colette admitted with pride that she was the original for Renée.

If her satisfaction in love—to borrow a thought from Léon Daudet—"must be accompanied by half-closed eyes in order not to distinguish too clearly the nature of the pleasure," Colette can none the less qualify as the perfect priestess of love, or rather, as she calls it, of the love of Love. Never indulging in abstract reflections, inspired by memories of perfumes, contacts, feelings, she "writes for the flesh alone." Owing to her acute intelligence of the senses, she understands all Léa's maternal voluptuousness when her young lover, settling himself for sleep, burrows his head into his accustomed resting place on her shoulder. She knows the full and sensuous meaning of "a long warm kiss, tranquil and not too poignant, the first thrill of which penetrating as far as the base of the spine, leisurely satiates itself before resolving into a slightly lethargic contentment." She can evoke the tense vigils of the jealous Renée, who almost listens to her sleeping lover's thoughts: "Your breathing is unequal and ceases altogether at the shock of two ideas. And when you turn your head upon the pillow I can hear your eyelashes scratch the silk in little hurried quivers." Familiar with all the lonely woman's craving for affection, she cries out: "Oh! to throw my arms about some neck, be it man or dog, any being who will love me!"

Colette has always communed more freely with the dumb

beast than with man. From her earliest years she has never been
without a cat, not to mention her dogs, squirrels, owls, leopards,
snakes, and a hundred other pets. Two of her books, *Dialogues
de bêtes* (1905) and *La Paix chez les bêtes* (1916), are devoted
to animals; while in *La Chatte* (1933), she relates the story of
a husband who forsakes his wife for the cat he loves with all
the tenderness of man for woman, a passion which the cat
reciprocates. "It is impossible to love at the same time animals
and man," she writes in *La Naissance du jour*. "As time goes
on, I become an object of suspicion to my fellow-men. If they
were my fellow-men, I should not be this object of suspicion."
Her second husband used to relate: "I always have the impression of being indiscreet when I enter a room and find my
wife alone with her animals. Some day she will retire into the
jungle." For further proof, Colette remarks playfully: "I no
longer have any desire to marry anyone, although I still dream
of someday espousing an enormous cat." She describes these
animals who frisk or purr their way throughout her books with
all the care, dignity, and sensuality that she bestows on human
characters, and we become as thoroughly acquainted with Kiki-
la-Doucette, or Toby-Chien as we do with Claudine or Chéri.
Do we not assist at their love-making and the most intimate moments of their feline existence? "It is the savage season of love
which severs us from all other joys and multiplies in diabolic
numbers our emaciated females in the garden. It is not that I
covet this slim, orange-brown one, flaming like a tulip, more
than I do that black, brilliant one, which resembles a wet eel.
Alas! it is not this one more than that one, or that other one.
But if I do not master all of them, my rivals will. Perhaps I
shall find in their bushy necks the marks my teeth left last
year. The nights of love are long, but I remain punctual, morose,
and vigilant at my post. I feel sad and more solitary than a
god, and an innocent desire for dawn, heat and rest torments

my weary vigil." This is not Don Juan speaking; it is only the monologue of a tomcat.

For Colette, animals are more than diverting playthings. They provide an outlet for emotion. "I am well aware that those sudden hungers of the sense of touch, those nervous meltings of the heart at the contact of a soft animal, reveal the overflowing of unutilized love, and I think that nobody undergoes this more profoundly than the old maid or the woman without a child." Colette is not an old maid and she has a daughter; nevertheless animals remain the greatest passion of her life. During the War her interest did not slacken, and in spite of a thousand other duties, she recounts in *Les Heures longues* (1918) how she used to visit the refuge where dogs were kept during their masters' absence at the front; indeed, her sympathy was equally divided between the *poilus* and the Red Cross dogs. During the war she wrote *La Paix chez les bêtes,* in which she explains that man was so busily engaged in killing man that for once he left the animals in peace.

Just as Colette attributes human traits to animals (for she makes it seem the most natural thing in the world that the heroine of *La Chatte,* which is a female cat, should suffer a woman's jealousy at the marriage of her master) her studies of women are so astonishingly real because she portrays their feline instincts. Colette sees, hears, feels, and acts in terms of animals. She makes hands "tremble like the paws of dogs who dream that they are running"; Chéri draws in his stomach "like a tomcat passing underneath a door"; Minne's mother packs trunks "with the activity of an ant conscious of a coming storm." When Colette speaks of hands, mouths, or hair, she is apt to forget and call them paws, muzzles, fur. She employs these similes in quick succession and writes in *L'Ingénue libertine:* "To calm the maddening tickle which spread like fire through his body at the contact of Minne's loosened hair, Antoine pushed her arms out wider, flattened himself against her, and rubbed as will an ignorant and excited young puppy. A snake-like spring pushed him back, and the slender wrists writhed in his fingers like the neck of a swan being strangled. 'You brute! Let me go!' He jumped back, and Minne remained against the door as if nailed there, a white gull with black mobile eyes."

Thus sensitive to the display of animal instincts, Colette believes that the impulsive physical gesture reveals the emotion more plainly than any number of words. In the catch of the breath, the flicker of an eyelash, the dilation of the nostril, the warmth of the cheek, her characters betray their feelings. Colette has no further need to analyze Léa's agitation when, after Chéri's first kiss, she lifts her hand "to rearrange her hair which had *not* been disturbed." As Colette's art matured, she found suggestion far more effective than close psychological analysis. Discarding all supplementary aids, she presents only the essential elements of her picture. The reader's interpretation will be gauged by his own capacity for emotional response. To say nothing of the greater brevity and directness of this method, her characters gain in heroism and intensity. Expatiating on her suffering, Renée seems whining and self-pitying. Léa, whose emotions are no less profound, inspires the greater sympathy because of her external reserve. When Jean in *L'Entrave* says "you ought to" and not "you should have," Renée realizes instantly that she is saved and that her rebellious lover means to take her back.

Colette is not one of those rare literary prodigies who merely have to sit before the writing-pad and let a masterpiece pour out. She achieved her glittering images and undulating phrases only after relentless dogged effort. "Oh! to be able to write!" she exclaims in *La Vagabonde*. "That signifies the long revery before the empty sheet, the play of the pen about a spot of ink, nibbling and clawing at the imperfect word, decorating it with

antennae and legs until it loses all legible appearance as a word
and becomes transmuted into a fantastic insect or drifts away
a butterfly." But Colette loved to write; one might almost say,
she loved in order to write. "Writing is the pleasure and the
torment of the idle. My need to jot down and paint my thought
becomes as keen at times as thirst in summer. It is something
like the itching of a scar that makes me take up my pen to play
this deceptive, perilous game of words, to capture and firmly
fasten under the double, pliant point the tickling, elusive, thrilling adjective." Caressing words, Colette indulges a further impulse of her sensuous nature and finds another fur to stroke.
When this caress becomes too obvious, it betrays the underlying effort. Rich and heavily ornate, her style sinks at times under
its very weight, and settings which should remain backdrops
are pushed upstage.

If Colette, as her admirers proclaim, is the greatest woman
novelist, she is at the same time a baffling personality for the
average Anglo-Saxon reader. Alternately attracted and repelled,
he must gaze in bewildering succession on Colette the housekeeper, the dressmaker, the devoted mother, the old maid with
her cat, the recluse, the actress, the voluptuary, and the faun.
For in Colette chastity and impurity are inextricably blended,
and she combines the naïve candor of the country child with
sophisticated licentiousness. How reconcile the fresh purity of
her descriptions of country life, her domestic tastes, her pity for
all suffering, with her unabashed, her total amorality? This an-
gelic perversity is disconcerting; it makes even such an emancipated spirit as André Gide call the reading of her books "a
delightful sin." For those who do not wish to sin, who do not
agree that nothing would be left Colette were love or the memories of love denied her, there remains the idyllic Colette of
La Maison de Claudine.

The Surrealists

THE more unhappy the era, the more need it has of *-isms,* and if Surrealism is a curious apparition in post-war literature, it is easily accounted for. A more appropriate name would have been Evasionism, for this was obviously an age which pleaded for escape. Never was there greater need for some value in the absolute, never was it more difficult to find one. The most sacred ideals had been shattered; there was doubt as to what was good or bad, beautiful or ugly, sane or mad. At a time when everything else had been shaken or annihilated, it was not to be expected that art alone should remain intact. The Surrealists were not men of genius, they were not even men of great intelligence. They were idealists, who scorned reality to seek some deeper essence, or, as their name implied, something superior to the real. Persuaded that this existed, they were groping around for it. Being intensely subjective, they were really looking for themselves, their first and greatest loss.

Some obscure law of averages decrees that each succeeding generation shall change its gods. A civilization continues just so far in any given direction; that culminating moment will arrive when it invariably swerves to a divergent one. Even without the revolutionizing fact of war, the pendulum would doubtless have swung back. By 1914 the cult of intelligence, graceful irony, and subtle estheticism had been pushed to its extreme limit by such men as Anatole France, Barrès, and Claudel. It was time for men "to fill their lungs with new air, to be coarse after so much elegance, violent after so much sweetness, simple after so much subtlety."

The art of painting was the first to undergo a change, for it was before the war, in 1907–1914, that Cubism imposed its grotesque standards. Wishing to simplify an art they felt had deteriorated through a wearisome virtuosity, painters such as Cézanne, Picasso, Braque, Derain, Duchamp, and Picabia—only to mention the most outstanding—ruthlessly eliminated what they deemed its unnecessary complications. Resorting to planes, cubes, and triangles, they sought to convey the essence rather than the objective aspect of their study. Unfortunately, far from achieving greater clarity, this excessive abstraction only contributed to their obscurity, for if, to the artist who conceives them, two lines are sufficient to convey an abbreviated conception of, let us say, a man, the uninitiated spectator has more difficulty in arriving at the same conclusion.

These artists instilled similar ambitions, and therefore similar faults, in their literary friends, and men like Guillaume Apollinaire, Max Jacob, Salmon, Carco, Cocteau, MacOrlan, Reverdy, and Cendrars became verbal Cubists. If Picasso is responsible for the practice of exhibiting his pictures upside down; if, when the legs of a model were too large to be attached in the customary manner to the human body, it was permissible to paint them in any free corner of the canvas, the word-pictures in imitation of such methods may be imagined. When musicians, artists, writers, and choreographers combined their efforts, and Stravinski, Picasso, Cocteau, and Diaghileff worked together, the cacophony was complete.

Finally, in an unholy moment, Dadaism was conceived. This was the neurotic child of the World War. Born in an age of incoherent obscurity of thought, of anarchy, negation, and abhorrence of tradition, Dadaism is a reflection of all these.

The story goes that Tristan Tzara, a Roumanian Jew, searching for a name to christen the new arrival, opened at random the Larousse dictionary and saw "dada," which means "horse," "hobby," "hobby-horse," or what you will, which was as good a name as any other for a movement its leaders were proud to proclaim meant absolutely nothing. All this occurred in 1916 at Zurich, where Tzara was living at the time and where the *Bulletin Dada* was first published. A short time later he installed himself at Paris, which, already prepared for Dadaism by such periodicals as *Sic* and *Nord-Sud,* was no longer shocked by any form of literary contortionism. Such tricks as the suppression of punctuation and of words essential to the normal structure of the sentence, had ceased to be a novelty. A review founded in 1919 by André Breton, Philippe Soupault, and Louis Aragon, and entitled in all seriousness *Littérature,* was conducted on dadaistic lines and boasted among its contributors such men as Paul Valéry, André Gide, Valery Larbaud, and Paul Claudel. The lesser but more radical luminaries were Apollinaire, Salmon, Eluard, Drieu La Rochelle, Péret, Ribemont-Sessaignes, Morand, Reverdy, Cendrars, and Cocteau, and in 1920 the *Bulletin Dada* changed its name but not its nature, and was henceforth called *Le Cannibale.* Dadaism had all the noisy publicity, if not the prestige, which marked the advent of Romanticism, some hundred years before. There were public demonstrations and countless manifestoes (Tzara himself wrote seven); there were hootings and fist fights, for that which cannot be established by reason must needs be buttressed by force.

If Dadaism was an outgrowth of Cubism, the aims of these two schools were entirely different. Where the Cubists aimed at being constructive, the Dadaists were destructive. The outcome, to be sure, was the same in either case, for they both resulted in complete unintelligibility, the Cubists through their abuse of intelligence, the Dadaists through their contempt for it. The spirit prompting Dadaism was doubt. It was not the beginnings of a new school, as its followers took pains to point out; it was the repudiation of all schools. The Dadaists destroyed merely to destroy, not without an eye to ephemeral notoriety. They were the last to know what they were seeking. "You do not understand what we are doing. Well, my dear friends, we understand still less" (Picabia). That is why the Dadaists needed so many manifestoes to convince themselves of their existence, so many tenets to argue that they had no tenets. "There is no Dada truth," says André Breton. "You have only to pronounce one sentence for the contradictory one to become Dada." Here are other Dada proclamations. "Every conviction is a malady" (Picabia). "Logic is always false" (Tzara). "Dada is a state of mind, a sort of artistic freethought, recognizing instinct only, condemning all previous explanations, and permitting the individual no self-control" (Breton). "The action of Dada is a permanent revolt of the individual against art, morals, and society; it aims at the abolishment of all dogmas, formulas and laws" (Breton). Tzara's recipe for a Dada poem: "Take a newspaper and some scissors. Choose from this paper an article having the length of the poem you desire; cut out all the words in this article and put them in a bag. Shake these up and draw them out at random, and this will be the order of their appearance in your poem. And lo!—you have become a writer of infinite originality and charming sensibility, although you must not hope, of course, to be understood by the vulgar crowd."

Born of anarchy, Dadaism was short-lived. Its followers early betrayed their lack of solidarity by indulging in tiffs and counter-accusations. Its very founder went back on it, and in 1922 Tzara writes: "The first to take leave of Dada was myself. Everybody knows that Dada means nothing and I parted company with it and myself as soon as I realized the full extent of this nothingness." Another to steal from the fold was Soupault, who says: "It is very difficult at the present moment to speak of the Dada movement. Nobody can know what it represented. Its face was mobile. For many of us it was a mirror, and that is doubtless why we were so desperately attached to it. Why not admit that we passionately loved the scandal it provoked. We wanted to shock and we did. We in turn were shocked by the public, for they actually sought to understand us. What madness! But I both loved and detested Dadaism. At one time I preferred to be called Philippe Dada rather than Philippe Soupault. But little by little we lost contact with ourselves and became our own slaves. At any rate, all is finished now, and I write novels."

Finding themselves without an *-ism,* the ex-Dadaists cast about rather desperately to find some new *raison d'être.* They finally hit on Surrealism which, while retaining some of the characteristics of Dadaism, was sufficiently original to be called a new school. In the first place, where Dadaism had been mainly a poetic movement, the Surrealists expressed themselves through prose. In spite of the fact that the Dadaists were furiously conscious of their impotence, in spite of their ironical argument that since nothing in life was real, positive, or demonstrable, all literature was unjustifiable, their own writings covered reams of paper. In comparison, the Surrealists wrote very little, and were chiefly preoccupied with formulating theories, outlining methods, issuing manifestoes, and insulting the world in general.

André Breton was the most important and belligerent of the Surrealists. It was he who found a name for the movement, became its theorist and formed a clan around it. He wrote its manifestoes (for as usual, the weaker the cause the more elaborate the propaganda); and persuaded a collaborator (Philippe Soupault) to launch the first experiment in Surrealism (*Les Champs magnétiques,* 1919). Breton was the sole editor of the revived *Littérature,* now turned Surrealist; and of a second review called *La Révolution surréaliste,* which, he boasted, was the most scandalous periodical in existence. His prose poem *Poisson soluble* (1924) is the most successful demonstration of the potentialities of his theories; while *Nadja* (1928) and *Les Vases communicants* (1930) strive to place the movement on a scientific basis.

Breton states that his oldest friends—and by this he means the oldest friends of Surrealism—are Soupault, Aragon, Eluard, Ernst, and Péret, to whom he adds the less tried and trusty Vitrac, Desnos, Delteil, Baron, and Picasso, to mention but a few of the men included in his list. Breton's passion is to enumerate his friends, who had a disconcerting fashion of changing and dwindling with each inventory. The dearest name was struck off when, shortly after the Armistice, the spectacular Jacques Vaché committed suicide. In order thoroughly to understand Breton, we must know the story of this eccentric friend whom he most admired and who exerted an enormous influence on his life.

In *Les Pas Perdus,* he relates their first encounter. This took place in 1916 when Vaché was recovering from a wound in a hospital where Breton was serving as an army doctor. A very elegant young man and a former student at the Beaux Arts, Vaché was skeptical of all literature, a disdain which increased his prestige in the eyes of the Dadaists. More than any other single force, Vaché, with his sense of "the theatrical uselessness of everything," his "umour" without an "h," impregnated the writers of this group with a philosophy of universal pessimism. His extraordinary conduct had all the earmarks of the "gratuitous act," so dear to Gide's heart. In spite of the fact that he was financially independent, he used to work as a river porter, to appear by night in the chic cafés, always wearing the smartest and most varied military uniforms. He obliged the young woman with whom he lived and whom, in spite of their platonic relation, he called his mistress, to remain humble and silent for hours on end in some corner of the room, only permitting her to serve tea to guests, whereupon by way of acknowledgment he would deign to kiss her hand. One evening in Paris during a theatrical performance which displeased him, he brandished a revolver in the hall and threatened to fire upon the audience. This odd and somber humor, which made him say, "I wish I were a trapper, or a bandit, a prospector, a hunter, a miner, or a sheep-shearer," an attitude defined by Soupault as a "terrible thirst for life at its strangest and its strongest," culminated in Vaché's final prank, his death in 1918 from an overdose of opium.

Breton was fascinated to an extraordinary degree by Vaché, and alludes to him constantly in the most tender and eulogistic terms. "A young man who, at the age of twenty-three, cast on the universe the most beautiful glance I knew, has mysteriously taken leave of us. It is easy for the world to claim that he was bored with life. In reality, he was the least weary and most subtle of us all. His good fortune was to have produced nothing, for he always spurned with his foot all works of art, which he looked upon as bullets retaining the soul after death. At the moment when Tzara was launching his first decisive Dada manifesto, Vaché was illustrating by his life that all philosophy is doubtful, and that everything one regards is false." Breton states that it was Vaché who prevented his desiring to be a poet or his being so absurd as to believe in a vocation. Indeed, most of the Surrealists disclaim all literary ambitions. When questioned as to why they write, Soupault, for one, replied: "I publish in order to seek mankind and for no other reason." Vaché was the very embodiment of the spirit of this age. In his blurred mind was firmly stamped one conviction: all effort is futile. Since the World War demonstrated the failure of reason, the sole alternative left to man, in order to attain absolute freedom, was to cease all effort. In abstaining from writing, in committing suicide,

Vaché for one was logical and courageous, for he put into action what his admiring friends merely dreamed about.

If Vaché died without a will, he left the testament of a letter in which he defines his literary opinions, and anticipates as though intuitively the nascent surrealistic school. He predicts that the new writers, totally indifferent to the censorship of logic, esthetics, or morality, will find an original and startling medium of expression through "a flamboyant collision of unusual words." Had he lived a few years longer, he would have witnessed the fulfilment of this extravagant prophecy. He would have seen his friends experimenting in hypnotism, automatic writing, dream talk, and abnormal psychology. These despairing pessimists thought that to enhance life one must escape from it at any cost; hence their recourse to the sphere of pure imagination, intuition, and the subconscious mind. "It is customary," explains Breton in his first manifesto of Surrealism, "to believe blindly that the life we see around us in our waking moments is the real one. But this is only the unstable phase of existence; and the man who dreams becomes increasingly dissatisfied with fate and those objects to which, either through indifference or the bent of his own activities, he finds himself reduced. Only by the play of the imagination can we lift this terrible interdiction and gain some inkling of what might really be ours." Freudian in their insistence on the inspiration of dreams, the Surrealists aver that only in our unconscious moments do we reveal our deepest and truest personality. At such times, being untrammeled by his reason, man's visions are more precious, and in fact the only ones on which true poetry should be based.

But since dreaming is an unconscious state which prevents us from noting our sensations, all this rich experience would be lost to humanity unless in our waking hours we induce a condition of mental passivity which permits us to hear these interior voices. In *Les Pas perdus*, Breton explains how he accomplished this. "In 1919 my attention was directed towards the more or less partial sentences which in the full solitude of the approach of sleep became perceptible to my mind, without its being possible to discover in these sentences a previous determination. Full of extraordinary images and of perfect grammatical construction, they appeared to me to contain certain poetic elements of the finest quality. It was only later that Soupault and I ventured voluntarily to induce the state of mind in which this would occur. It was sufficient to exclude the exterior world, and after two months' effort, these sentences would reproduce themselves with such extraordinary rapidity that we were reduced to abbreviations in order to record them. *Les Champs magnétiques* was the first fruit of this discovery, and since then I have never ceased to be persuaded that nothing of value can be said or done except by following this magic dictation." Demonstrating that by allowing the hand to trace at random the words suggested by the subconscious mind, a multitude of sudden and accidental conflicts between words and ideas would result, the Surrealists insisted that this joining of delightfully audacious images was capable of opening unexplored horizons unfettered by banal associations. This, then, is Surrealism: a certain psychic automatism corresponding most nearly to a state of dreaming in which are recorded, either by writing or some other means, the innermost functioning of the mind. Some may prefer the more complicated definition which Aragon as a Surrealist draws up: "Surrealism denies the real to move in the unreal; denies in turn the unreal; and this double negation, far from resulting in the affirmation of the real, confounds it with the unreal, but goes beyond these two ideas in seizing a middle term where both are denied and affirmed, conciliated and contained."

Aragon concedes that all surrealistic inspiration is not of equal value; its value will depend on the force and originality of the person who experiments. It is not sufficient to induce the state of dreaming; the dream must be well reported, and its form and substance good. Not every hand is capable of transcribing what the mind perceives; this is reserved for the perfect master of words.

In spite of their great expectations, the Surrealists were obliged to admit that their results were at times discouraging. Breton explains how he reëstablishes his serenity: "If a sentence causes me a momentary disappointment, I am very careful not to change or perfect it later. The slightest infraction on my initial impulse would be fatal, and I wait until the following sentence to redeem my faults. The groups of words which follow one upon the other constitute the greatest solidarity, and it is not for me to favor one group at the expense of another. I wait for something marvelous to intervene—and it does!" Apparently the Surrealists, like the negro whom Soupault describes in one of his novels, live in constant expectation of a miracle. While waiting for one, Breton, a specialist in neurology, has other consolations. When not concentrating on poetry, that domain of the marvelous and the artificial, he can devote himself to a scientific investigation of dreams and the world of the psychiatrist, a study as fascinating, it appears, as the discovery of a new vice.

For the Surrealists, in their attempt to enrich the field of consciousness, had recourse to the madman's world. Although only Aragon and Breton were trained neurologists, most of the others in this group were ex-soldiers and had had the opportunity to observe the mental states of many war victims who, if not altogether insane, were in some form or other irremediably unbalanced. But the Surrealists, far from regarding mental derangement as a misfortune, looked upon it as a privilege. Who but the insane, asks Breton, can draw comfort from their imagination? In what other condition is man entirely innocent and scrupulously honest? "See how madness took form at times and lasted. Was it not in the company of insane men that Columbus

set out to discover America?" And taking violent issue with the
alienists, whom he reproaches for abusive treatment of their
patients, Breton believes that these victims should assassinate
the doctors and regain their liberty. So in *L'Immaculée Conception*, Breton and Eluard attempt to simulate in words the
various mental abnormalities, and oppose to the narrow field of
waking consciousness the greater activities which delirium affords. However, the Surrealists overlook the important fact that
in order to record the ravings of the mad, it is necessary for the
recorder to be sane, and that no sane person can ever completely
experience the aberrations of the insane. Just as Paul Valéry,
who believes that no one must be more wide awake than the person who wishes to transcribe his dreams, says: "If you wish to
reproduce accurately the fantasticality and the inconsistency of
the feeble dreamer that you have just been, if you wish to pursue
to its depths that pensive fall of the soul, comparable as it is to
a dead leaf through the vague immensity of the memory, do not
flatter yourself that you will be able to succeed in it without an
attention pushed to its extreme limits, the masterpiece of which
will be to take unawares that which only exists at the expense
of this attention."

Claiming that the "marvelous" is always beautiful, the Surrealists argued that fairy tales should be written not only for
children but for adults. Aragon's *Anicet* (1921) is one of these.
In this extravagant fantasy, the young hero meets a curious individual named Arthur (generally supposed to be Arthur Rimbaud), in a hotel dining room where, though indulging in a
Barmecide feast before empty plates and glasses, he evinces the
most evident signs of gastronomic enjoyment. Such a man has
evidently a different conception of existence from the average
mortal. Indeed, Aragon's chief amusement is to interpret the
physical world with a complete disregard for the laws of time
and space. "I could say that I was born," explains this Arthur,

"if such a term were not inaccurate in representing an action as in the past instead of a fact independent of duration." In like manner, Arthur liberates himself from what he calls "the lie of perspective," and imagines on a single plane that which the ordinary person is obliged to place on several. This metaphysical anarchy enables him to perceive several objects simultaneously, brings the Sahara Desert to the Place de la Concorde, grows a forest about the Opéra. If Japanese dancing mice are conscious of only two dimensions, Aragon proposes four or five. His heroine Mirabelle, who is more of an abstraction than a human being, is invested with the power of ubiquity, and able to vanish into space at will. Believing that society is circumscribed and thwarted through the obligation to follow conventional codes, Aragon proposes complete emancipation of the spirit for the attainment of a broader and more philosophic point of view. Therefore his hero Anicet murders, steals, and is unhampered by all moral inhibitions. Indeed Aragon, who has been called "the terrorist" of Surrealism, would have liked to destroy all ethics, philosophy, and religion, and substitute the life of illusion, the only true one.

But Aragon, like most of the Surrealists, refused to be quoted or understood. In fact, Breton stated that to read a book for the purpose of comprehending it is a sign of naïve simplicity, and that poets should do everything in their power to conceal their meaning. This is a criterion of art which automatically crowns the Surrealists with laurels, for, pages on end, their works are veiled in all the obscurity of night. Some of their riddles are: "the bargain sale of soapy streams"; "the selling of crimes and odorless tears"; "stiff stalk of Suzanne inutility especially village of flavor with a church of lobster"; "oozing cathedral upper vertebrae." When hundreds of such sentences are thrown together in wild disorder, it is a delirium of words. an orgy of nonsense.

However, it cannot be denied that the Surrealists occasionally achieved poetic beauty, the "flamboyant collision of words" of which Vaché spoke. This produces such haunting imagery as: "the lace of sensations"; "orange rain with underside of fern leaves"; "raindrops resembling the transparent eggs of humming-birds." In moments of forgetfulness, the Surrealists could even be coherent: "What saint with apron of roses had made this divine extract to flow in the veins of stones?" Or: "The dead elm and the bright green catalpa are the only objects which sigh in the untamed stars' avalanche of milk." When Breton abandoned this so-called automatic writing—the authenticity of which is not above suspicion—for his expository style, he changed from total incomprehensibility to what is almost worse, a monotonous and heavy-handed pedantry. From a purely literary point of view, Aragon was undoubtedly the most able of the Surrealists, and if in substance his *Anicet* adhered to surrealistic principles, in form, at least, it is as pure as any eighteenth-century model.

By the year 1928, as we learn from Breton's *Second manifeste du surréalisme,* this movement had reached a new stage in its evolution. Now more than a diverting game of words, it aimed at social and moral revolution. Many of its earlier supporters were in lively disagreement as to the anti-religious and anti-social activities towards which Breton was directing them. "The simplest thing for the Surrealists to do," writes the irascible Breton, "would be to go into the street and shoot at random on the crowd. Anything would be legitimate to ruin the established ideas of family, church, and fatherland." As a literary movement Surrealism was on the wane. Breton produced two new and tedious books. The first, *Nadja* (1928), is autobiographical, and supplied with authentic names and dates, even to photographs of the scenes and characters. It describes Breton's chance encounter in a café with a young woman of mediumistic powers, its thesis being that coincidences are not the result of hazard but the proof of an occult universe which only indifference prevents us from perceiving. *Les Vases communicants* (1932) continues the investigation of psychic phenomena, and studies the relation of dreams to real life. Analyzing in detail his own dreams, Breton reviews a certain period in his life characterized by unusually irrational conduct, in order to demonstrate that mental disorder is only a dream in action.

The Surrealists are significant not so much for their literary output as for the state of mind which prompted them to write. One psychologist, Janet, admits the philosophic interest of the movement, but condemns the skepticism inherent in a doctrine which maintains that reality is ugly on principle. Another doctor, de Clerambault, classifies these men as *Procédistes,* meaning that they relied on formulas which automatically produced the abridged and conventional effect desired, and which spared them the painful necessity of thinking. Men who follow such a system, he informs us, are invariably characterized by laziness and pride.

Mental laziness may well have been responsible for much of their disorder. "To doubt all or to believe all," says Henri Poincaré, "are two equally convenient expedients for escaping the onus of reflection." Breton, for one, was never a partisan of the intellect. Scorning erudition or culture, he says that his own education was of the most mediocre description, and that he regrets even the few years he did devote to it. Aragon went even further: "Fool stupidity is my one possession and I mean to keep it."

As to the arrogant pride of the leaders of Surrealism, perhaps this was a natural attitude in men who waged, as they delighted to assert, "a war of independence." Soupault announced that "one and one make four, if I decree it." "The planets and the stars of first magnitude are as nothing compared to us," assert the co-authors of *Les Champs magnétiques.* "In the schools of the state," writes Aragon, "children are put in intellectual vases in order to subjugate them to their vices. All that is lowest and most inhuman is taught and cultivated there: Horace, Virgil, Montaigne, Corneille, Molière, Descartes, Spinoza, Tennyson, Schiller, Voltaire, Napoleon, Flaubert, Balzac, Auguste Comte, and Daudet. And see what smoke escapes from all this mess: Anatole France, Marcel Proust, and Charles Maurras. To all of this tradition of what is beautiful and proper, we Surrealists oppose our own conceptions, as infernal as they are."

Much should be pardoned the Surrealists, for they were young and most unhappy. Perhaps, indeed, they were lonely: Breton states that he used to leave his door open at night in the hope that in the morning he would awake to find some unknown bedfellow by his side. "Despair" is the word most constantly on their lips. "We two," write Breton and Soupault in *Les Champs magnétiques,* "have no other refuge than these cafés where we meet to drink. Our eyes move aimlessly and hopelessly about; we can no longer even think. When words escape from our twisted lips and we laugh, the passers-by turn around to stare, and rush frightened to their homes." Stifled by the ennui of living, they resembled the heroes in Soupault's novels, who wonder at times how they can possibly put in another day. These feverish, discontented spirits found in writing or, as Aragon called it, "blackening paper," their most effective solution for killing time. Breton said that only with ink and paper before him could he keep his mind awake. Referring to Surrealism as "our adventure," they huddled together for mutual protection and admiration. One of Soupault's devices for provoking his friends' applause was to canvass various apartment houses and inquire if he, Philippe Soupault, lived there. "Nor would Soupault have been astonished," says Breton, evidently much impressed, "if he had received an affirmative reply; he would have

gone immediately to ask admittance at his own door." Soupault
at least had the saving grace of frankness, and confessed: "Many
of us would have been only too willing to die provided we could
make people talk of us." However, according to Paul Valéry:
"The desire to cause astonishment is the most natural and readily
conceivable of all desires in writers, and permits the most insignificant reader to decipher the extremely simple secret of many
a surprising work."

The best-advised among the Surrealists eventually realized
their folly in having identified themselves with this tempestuous
movement. Soupault, for one, abandoned it in self-defense, and
first putting order into his life, which he calls his chief concern,
then into his style, he now writes in simple and naïve vein. Aragon has been logical enough to become a militant Communist.
His recent *Les Cloches de Bâle* is a brilliant book, in which he
announces that he will henceforth sing the praises of the modern
woman. Although Breton to all practical intents and purposes
has also retreated into Communism, he still maintains that there
is an abyss separating the Marxian revolution of the moment and
the revolution of the poet. The eternal revolt against man's condition incorporates but far surpasses the objective of mere materialistic amelioration, and this he calls Surrealism.

Jean Cocteau

CRITICS should be grateful to Cocteau for the splendid opportunity given them to exercise their special talent. Any man of letters who writes a pantomime (*Le Bœuf sur le toit*), names a café after it, and then plays jazz there, invites familiarity. He is vulnerable on so many sides that it is merely a question of which ones to attack. There is Cocteau the literary acrobat, the faddist, the snob, the eternal sophomore, the egotist, the coquet, and the opium addict. This last presents the special problem of whether we are dealing with this author in his rational moments or in his opium dreams. What faults, what virtues, may be attributed to his vice, or, on the other hand, to his periods of disintoxication? He himself professes to be ashamed of the books he wrote when not under the influence of drugs.

He has written some twenty books. After sifting the chaff— two volumes of verse; three or four collections of miscellaneous essays; as many more volumes of choreographic and theatrical pieces; five or six albums of cartoons and drawings; even a "talkie" film—there remain three novels: *Le Grand Ecart, Thomas l'Imposteur,* and *Les Enfants terribles,* Cocteau's rather slim credentials for serious literary consideration. A label is often a dubious guide to the actual content of a package, so Cocteau's classification of all his work as poetry—whether authentic verse or trivial prose utterance—is not a trustworthy advertisement of his wares. If the will always fathered a deed, Cocteau would long ago have been a poet, for he has striven to be one all his life.

His efforts began as a young man who, "charged with the electricity of poetry, but bewildered by doubtful praise and stiffened with pride," found himself "incapable of forging a transmitting process," and obliged "to turn over and over again on the same spot, like a sick person trying to fall asleep." Relating how, after five years on the march, he knocked at the stern Muses' door, he says: "It is a mistake to suppose that you will be very warmly received; these Muses never ask you to sit down, but point in silence to a tightrope. Up there, suspended in space, so many precautions are necessary in order not to break one's neck, that this became my unique preoccupation." It was Cocteau's misfortune to have the aspirations but not the genius of the poet, so that his public, though fascinated spectators of much brilliant footwork as he teetered on the tightrope, were never permitted to witness a successful crossing to the other side. Indeed, most critics made short work of him as a poet, and laughed at his pretensions in mistaking literary fireworks for genuine inspiration. Rousseaux calls them "rockets failing to explode," "hollow nuts," "soap bubbles." The irony of his situation did not escape Cocteau, for he says: "I can imagine that the gestures of a man swaying over the jaws of death must be extremely diverting. At any rate, I was invited in all good faith to become a member of the Academy of Humor."

Feverishly desirous of being admired and loved, Cocteau mingled with keen-witted artists and dilettanti; he hobnobbed with such celebrities as Satie, Stravinski, Picasso, Milhaud, Poulenc, and Gide. Having become a fashionable figure, like most pets he soon degenerated into a harmless satellite, hypnotized by these more brilliant lights. His vanity made him desire to become a leader; his obsequious nature and lack of true originality condemned him to be a perpetual follower. Rousseaux compares him to a "sort of female drum-major, the soul of whose regiment has passed into her veins. She loves the goal towards which the soldiers are advancing with a fervor equal to their own; her reactions spring from theirs. It is in this manner that Cocteau furnished clever replicas in turn of Edmond Rostand, Robert de Montesquiou, Madame de Noailles, and Guillaume Apollinaire. Each time these artists created something, the Muse of Cocteau was prepared to receive the germ and increase with a few bastards the legitimate family of her lover. Cocteau could thus delude himself into believing that he also was a creator."

Many of Cocteau's sharpest thrusts are boomerangs. In an imprudent moment he said: "Every man has a monkey seated on his right shoulder and a parrot perched upon his left." He began to crave notice and be fêted as an artist at a time when the prevailing note in art was incoherence. Any irrelevant array of words in literature, of sounds in music, of color in painting, was welcomed as a reaction against discipline, and therefore worthy of exhibition. This resulted in a matching of wits; and Cubism, Dadaism, and Surrealism enjoyed in turn a fleeting triumph. These fads encouraged whatever talents an artist had for caricature or the grotesque; they made a strong appeal to Cocteau— or rather, to the monkey and the parrot seated on his shoulder. These two seized eagerly the prevailing formulas and produced *Les Mariés de la Tour Eiffel, Antigone, Le Potomak,* and other fantastic works. In order to create unusual effects in his theatrical productions, he resorted to the use of megaphones and phonographs. He employed supers to shout the names of various advertisements, and rounds of "Pear's Soap" resounded while the members of the orchestra filed in. Here is the author's own description of the principal actors in *Parade,* the cubistic ballet composed in collaboration with Satie and Picasso: "A Chinaman who produces an egg from his pigtail, eats it, finds it again in the toe of his shoe, spits fire, burns himself, stamps out the fire, etc."; "a little girl who mounts a race horse, rides a bicycle, imitates Charlie Chaplin, chases a thief with a revolver, boxes, dances rag-time, is shipwrecked, rolls on the grass, and buys a kodak." The music, equally ultra, was calculated to supply an atmosphere of steam whistles, typewriters, and airplanes. "Reality alone has the power to arouse emotions," he explains. "Too long have we been led astray through a fatal preoccupation with beauty. Art must be brought down to earth and suggest facts; we need art upon which we can walk and sit, art that we can eat, like bread. We have had too much music in which one lies and soaks as in a warm bath; too many hammocks, garlands, gondolas." Cocteau was far from being the only one to follow these fallacious standards, for many others, in striving for greater simplicity and terseness, were thus despiritualizing art. They overlooked the fact that in removing art from literature, they also extracted the poetry, the very thing they were so eager to produce.

If Cocteau never completed an act upon the tightrope, at least he never tumbled to the ground. His ability to sense danger enabled him to rectify his mistakes before they became irreparable. When he saw that it was futile to continue one experiment, he immediately tried his hand at another. Thus each of his works was in the nature of a début and accompanied with all its risks. In this manner he essayed the ballet, neo-classical drama, Shakespearean plays, the circus, the music-hall, Dadaism, and, most recently, the "talkies." He has sought inspiration in cubist painting, modernistic music, and jazz. He has imitated Gide, Barrès, Morand, and even his own disciple, Radiguet. Claiming that there is an underlying unity in all his work, he says: "Each of my books is only the continuation of an original drawing. My friends, who are looking over my shoulder, see what my pen is tracing without understanding what this is meant to represent. You have only to begin by drawing the feet first and everybody's calculations are upset. When the work is almost finished, you put in the eye and suddenly the manikin appears. The function of my last book will doubtless be to add the eye." Then, turning to scourge those who have been so undiscerning as to have failed to detect this unity, he adds: "I can picture my critics comfortably seated to view my theatrical pieces and finding nothing but disorder there. Critics are always clamoring for poets to produce a serious work. Let them wait! Aside from the fact that this word 'work' has become exceedingly distasteful to me, I can imagine nothing more deplorable than a poet who fulfills the promise of his talent."

Believing the vulgar crowd incapable of appreciating his art, Cocteau adopted an increasingly supercilious attitude towards both critics and public. Indeed, in no other writer is the pleasing virtue of modesty so sadly missed. More optimistic than Stendhal, who prophesied that his works would only be appreciated a half century later, Cocteau writes: "I give the world twenty years before the poetry contained in my *Mariés de la Tour Eiffel* receives its just appraisal. Until then, this work will only rank as a rather feeble comic dialogue. Its aim is too true, its weapon too perfect, to be understood at present." According to this prediction, 1940 should be his year of glory. The trouble is that the more Cocteau expatiates on the beauty and subtlety of his work, the more the reader's attention is directed towards their absence.

In all justice, it must be admitted that Cocteau is equally enthusiastic about his friends' achievements. His life has been a series of infatuations for various artists, writers, and musicians, whose quarrels he assumes and whose successes he applauds. He has always been an ardent impresario for talented young men, and it is through Cocteau's efforts that the youthful Radiguet was launched, as well as the less worthy Marcel Desbordes with his *J'adore*. His life was darkened by the death of many of his most intimate friends, and in his *Lettre à Maritain* he writes: "Seven times God spared my life without my realizing it at the time. God would send me friends only to withdraw them. The line was cast seven times and pulled back without taking me. Do not think that God was exterminating youth; he simply wanted to create more angels." "Heaven's gloves," as he calls these friends, they were merely "lent to earth for a short time and then called back to the skies unsullied."

Was it to relieve these sorrows that Cocteau sought solace, first in opium, and then in God? Or was God only a different kind of drug? We know that Max Jacob recommended the communion wafer to him as a substitute for aspirin. Rousseaux suggests that it more nearly resembled an aphrodisiac. According to Cocteau, his conversion was due to the fascinating personality of a certain priest. "Father Charles produced the same effect upon me as Stravinsky and Picasso. In revealing to me that masterpiece, the Holy Communion, he furnished me with evidence of God's existence." Asserting that art for art's sake and art for the masses are equally absurd, Cocteau, in his latest phase, proposes art for God.

If we shut out the gaudy spotlights he loves to direct on himself, a steadier luminary reveals the child who still lingers there. Familiar with all the obscure rites of the adolescent mind, he shows himself a master when he writes of the world of growing children. It is because of this theme that his three novels constitute his finest work.

Since children, as Cocteau points out, are prone to become silent in the presence of their elders, it is difficult to observe the functioning of their instincts, qualified variously by him as animal and vegetable. The average grown-up sees only the gestures of these young bodies, their souls he can never hope to penetrate. It is probable that everyone has passed through this period of adolescent dreaming, varying in intensity according to the quality of the individual imagination. Once an outcast from this enchanted realm, the Olympian has only faint recollections of his former dream-world, flashes sufficient to remind him, however, that a few drops of its magic fluid still course in his veins. Cocteau has retained more of these drops than the average person. Never completely outgrowing his childhood, he has kept the ability to impart its mysteries. He explains that *Les Enfants terribles* really deals with grown-up people situated in a period much more remote than childhood, "a sillier, vaguer zone, more discouraging and full of shadows." If he chooses youthful characters, it is because he finds in the disordered mind of the adolescent a nearer approach to his own chaotic spirit. In evoking the nebulous plane midway between dreams and reality, Cocteau qualifies temporarily as the poet he claims to be.

His young people never seem to belong completely to our earthly planet. Jacques, in *Le Grand Ecart,* is described as a youth who is "partly light, and partly shadow." "One half of the world reposes, the other works. But from the dreaming half emanates a mysterious force which counteracts the waking element." As a result of this strange interfusion, Jacques, whose desires are as vague as they are deep rooted, somnambulates through life. An impressionable schoolboy who becomes involved in a sordid love-affair, and who, when disillusioned, attempts to kill himself; the story is banal enough. More interesting is the hero's evolution into a sophisticated but melancholy young man, who has learned that in order to live one must conform to the world's ways, even though one has no further interest in it.

Thomas l'imposteur is the story of a sixteen-year-old boy who at the outbreak of the World War is seen posing, more by accident than premeditation, as the nephew of an illustrious general. Under these false colors, the guileless young impostor wins the love of a girl of patrician blood, becomes indifferent to his conquest, craves adventure, and finally dies on No Man's Land. He is represented as living his lie so completely that everyone, including himself, forgets that it is a lie, by which Cocteau means to show that it is impossible for youth to sin. A phantom slipping through a world of facts, Thomas is a creation in which make-believe and reality are so subtly interwoven that they become identical.

Becoming more and more absorbed in the study of the adolescent mind, Cocteau penetrates to greater depths in his last novel, *Les Enfants terribles*. Here the young people are portrayed as leading an inner life completely independent of the outside world. Since verisimilitude is the least of Cocteau's pre-occupations, it is wiser to accept without question the extraordinary circumstances enabling this quartet of children, of whom only two are brother and sister, to live together pell-mell in a sort of Noah's Ark in the heart of modern Paris. The puzzled reader learns of the strange game of "departing" which these young people have invented. Although its moves are never very clearly defined, the goal consists in inducing a state of semi-consciousness fraught, apparently, with mysterious delights for the players. In this condition, which resembles closely that caused by dream-producing drugs—indeed, Cocteau is said to have written this book during one three-week period when he was under the influence of opium—the children feel themselves immersed in a sort of blissful twilight where they seem to be dominating time and space. The fact that they eventually grow up and marry does not fundamentally alter their strange natures, although the resultant crystallization of their emotions renders them less responsive subjects for their game. In the end, this hobby proves to be more than an innocent, youthful frolic: its rituals neglected, it reclaims its faithless worshippers through death.

If we accept Cocteau's definition of a literary masterpiece, "a dictionary in disorder," his works fall all too naturally under this heading. They must be accepted and enjoyed as a series of glittering and rapidly moving scenes developed by means of clever verbal juggling. Surprisingly enough, he disclaims all mannerisms, and maintains that he writes with "style" and not "a style." Whatever he calls it, his books have charm, even in those passages, unfortunately all too frequent, which seem devoid of meaning. His ability to impart a light touch to everything, he defines as "a clean vivacity." Straining his thought of all superfluous elements, he likes to distill its purest essence. His novels give the impression of having been systematically shortened from an earlier, fuller draft of which only every third or fourth line has been retained. This leaves but the skeleton of a structure, mere topic sentences, which most writers would have developed further. While these short cuts give intensity and speed, they deprive the reader of much necessary information. Cocteau seems first to conceive his aphorism, then invent a character on which to pin it. Caught in some characteristic pose and concisely illumined by an image or an anecdote, these people are delineated by means of instantaneous flashlights. Cocteau introduces a simile less to supplement the thought, than to be the thought, from which the breathless reader must extract as best he can the individual psychology. He says, for instance, that "a poet must swallow a locomotive and bring up a pipe"; or "Venice by night is an amorous negress who had died in her bath wearing all her cheap jewels"; or "Maritain's body is a formula of politeness thrown quickly over his soul to receive his friends." When not exclusively preoccupied with startling paradoxes, and witty, if superficial epigrams, Cocteau reveals himself as a remarkably keen analyst. Although he can never resist exaggeration nor the desire to be spectacular, he is capable of such penetrating criticism as this of Barrès: "He is one of those people who fear to act without a precedent. He turns back ten times before his jump. . . . A strong man jumps a river without taking into consideration the possibility that it is too wide.

A long time afterwards he is admired for this. Barrès only jumps over rivers when the experiment has already been made. But this is an exaggeration. A bridge has been set up to commemorate some famous leap; so, let us say, Barrès hesitates where to cross, and finally decides on the spot where the leap took place. In the middle of the bridge he stops; he is dreaming. He is touched by the thought that his decision follows so closely on the path of that former glorious one, and he is moved to tears."

It is in such light and mordant comment that Cocteau reveals his special gifts. To use his own dart against Barrès, he is not a swan, but a "bright-colored duck" who from his happy little pond casts longing eyes upon the lake.

Julien Green

AMERICA follows with special interest the career of her brilliant expatriate, Julien Green. Not that there remains overmuch of the American in a man who was born in France and who, except for three years of study at the University of Virginia, has always lived abroad. However, neither his choice of a foreign home nor the adoption of French as his literary medium can alter the fact that he is an American. With admiration mingled with pride we have marveled at his precocity and rejoiced in his rapid rise to fame. This came when he was a young man in his twenties, for with *Adrienne Mesurat,* his second novel, he was pronounced a master. The recipient of various literary awards, included in every list of the best contemporary French novelists, he was more generously praised in France than many a talented French writer. If, ironically enough, he was known to most of his countrymen only through translation, at least they hastened to read him. Nor was his American vogue solely dependent on his availability in English, for even the average Anglo-Saxon linguist could read this simple, unassuming French with comparative ease. The fact that it does present so little difficulty suggests that Green's is not a distinctively Gallic medium, even if the Americanisms in his early works were not additional evidence. Indeed, it would be interesting to know whether some of his early work was not written first in English. At present, with five novels to his credit, he has acquired a much more fluent style, although even now, Green prudently limits his aspiration to what he calls "invisible prose," where thought, not phrase, is given precedence.

He was particularly suited to the American mind from another point of view. Retaining, as it were, one last vestige of his Anglo-Saxon descent, he is one of the most reticent of authors when his subject is sex. Where writers such as Henri de Régnier would have alienated American readers by their lewdness, Julien Green covertly implies but never frankly confronts the physical aspect of love, and so escapes unscathed. He is more communicative on other and no less unlovely themes, but since he stresses the passions and never passion, the most puritanical can plunge with confident relish into this world of thwarted lives, blind injustice, and ferocious hate.

For Green has a somber imagination, and believes that happy people have no story, that the ugly offers greater interest than the beautiful. At first this attitude might have been attributed to his youth, for many a young author, fresh from Baudelaire and the Realists, adopts a morbid point of view. But since Green is now thirty-four and still sees black, it must be assumed that his point of view is adult and natural to him. If it were only a question of settings, his are neutral enough. Unfortunately, he must people these backgrounds, and he too frequently peoples them with monsters. Placing his characters in the most commonplace surroundings, he excels in endowing them with an abnormality of feeling and a violence of passion all the more dramatic because of their everyday background.

From the first, abnormal psychology had a fascination for him, and his youthful stories, *Le Voyageur sur la terre, Les Clefs de la mort, Christine* and others, depicted morbid, sensitive young people afflicted with hallucinations and leading isolated, misdirected lives. This interest in the so-called "idiot fringe" was soon to manifest itself on a larger scale in his novels. In the earliest of these, *Mont-Cinère* (1926), named after the estate in Virginia where his characters live, Green introduces us to his first really full-fledged monsters. A widow, whose economical habits have grown with inexorable intensity into an all-absorbing mania, Mrs. Kate Fletcher subjects her daughter, a neurotic girl of fifteen, to such cruel and pointless privations—for in possessing Mont-Cinère this family is far from poor—that the child becomes deranged. Mrs. Fletcher renders equally miserable the old age of her mother, who is ill and forced to share her roof. With such a deplorable family life as a background, this dismal tale recounts the daughter's unnatural proposal of marriage to their ex-gardener, a young widower with a child, by means of whom she plans to usurp her mother's place; and her incendiary burning of Mont-Cinère upon discovering that the gardener husband means to assert his mastery.

Since the infinitely more mature *Adrienne Mesurat* was to appear just one year later, the crudity of this earlier novel is all the more outstanding. Far from developing convincing characters in *Mont-Cinère,* Green has done little more than supply *leitmotifs* which, in spite of their insistent repetition, are not sufficient to create the impression of reality or even of remote plausibility. It is not enough to remind the reader at every page that Mrs. Fletcher is a sort of female Harpagon and that the daughter has an equal lust for possession. By concentrating on a single facet of their personality to the point of ignoring all other traits, he has created unbalanced characters for whom there is neither law nor reason.

As a foreshadowing of his future work, however, this early story presents several points of interest, for the author is already experimenting with certain themes which in his later novels he develops with greater subtlety and skill. At first it may be surprising to discover that husband and wife, mother and daughter, in not only one but several generations, should so completely detest one another. With each succeeding book, we learn to expect this family-hate *motif,* which eventually becomes inseparably linked with the name of Julien Green. In the three hundred pages of *Mont-Cinère,* there is not a civil word exchanged. On the rare occasions when these people do converse, their speech is abrupt and churlish, suggestive of a lower stratum of society than that with which this book is dealing and which, for lack of a better name, must be called the "gentry." The adverbs selected to qualify their conversation are reduced to "briefly," "dryly," "curtly," superfluous reminders in view of the words they utter. It is possible to believe in the acidity prevailing between members of Green's family groups, but where the outside world is involved such bad manners and disregard for social amenities become increasingly shocking and improbable.

With *Adrienne Mesurat,* Green revealed the full measure of his talent. Turning to France, and the small provincial town where the Mesurat family lives, Green is perfectly at home. Although the heroine herself is not a monster, she is surrounded by them. Persecuted by a tyrannical father and a dour, malignant older sister, the embittered Adrienne has lived until her eighteenth year in a coma of unrelieved and apathetic boredom. Into the dreary vacuum of this existence comes the chance encounter with the new doctor who lives across the street. This first momentary glimpse—for no words have been exchanged—is sufficient to inspire the lonely girl with an irrational and tenacious passion. From this point on, everything and everyone conspire against her—but chiefly Julien Green. It required no little ingenuity to make things go so incredibly wrong. In a fit of hysteria she pushes her father down a flight of stairs, and causes his instant death; she is blackmailed by an adventuress, a neighbor who has divined her guilt; and her love is rejected by the doctor. Her last hope shattered, there snaps what little remains of her already tottering reason. If the author's success is to be gauged by the measure of suffering he has created, this book is a grim fulfilment of his fondest hopes. We may question why he wished to place his heroine on this rack of pain, but his genius as a torturer is beyond dispute.

To offer still further proof, he wrote *Léviathan* (1929), a novel of greater variety and range, though inferior to *Adrienne Mesurat* as a work of art. This reference in the title to the biblical monster Leviathan does not belie the nature of the story. Some avenging spirit pursues the hero Guéret, who, as a result of his unrequited passion for a village girl, leaves murder, rape, suicide, and insanity in his trail. A curse was also placed on the pathetic little Angèle, the laundress whom he mutilates, though why, as a public prostitute, she steadfastly refused his love, is never satisfactorily explained. No less unfortunate is the frustrated and vindictive Mme Grosgeorge, the familiar Green monster, who "having detested her child from the moment she felt it struggling within her entrails, darkened its earliest years with uncalled-for punishments," a woman so inhuman, the author informs us, that "her nature produced nothing in which poison was not in some way mingled, warping her simplest feelings and corrupting every affection at its source." Of the plot, always Green's special bugbear, suffice it to say that in spite of its skilful presentation, the level hardly rises above that of a harrowing melodrama.

After the publication of *Léviathan,* Green announced that with these first three novels he had completed his observation of a certain phase of life and would henceforth write in a different vein. However, in his next novel, *Epaves* (1932), which is the least effective of all his books, aside from the shifting of the scene from the provinces to Paris, and the application of less violent colors, there is little indication of a change of heart. The inevitable obsession is still present—cowardice this time—and the familiar family dissension. The story itself is very simple: a young married couple have never loved each other since their wedding night; the woman who really loves this faint-hearted and fatuous man is his wife's older unmarried sister, who shares their apartment, and who, though only thirty-one, is described as "a shriveled old maid with wrinkles"; the wife meanwhile is meeting secretly another man whose sole and rather incredible attraction is his squalor. Where *Adrienne Mesurat* and *Léviathan* stimulated interest through the steady progression of horror built up around a central theme, in *Epaves,* where little happens and where there is no crescendo to a tragic culmination, all that remains are three eccentric and rather silly people arbitrarily housed within a single apartment. The most significant comment is that except for certain naïve and improbable episodes, the story quickly fades from memory.

In Julien Green's latest novel, *Le Visionnaire* (1934), a much more successful work, he reverts once more to his favorite setting of the province, and chooses for his hero a forlorn young man who finds himself thwarted and unhappy. Ugly, timid, servile, and dying of tuberculosis, he seeks relief from reality by immersing himself in a world of dreams. But his sufferings have so permeated his subconscious being that the visions he evokes are no less horrible than the life he is striving to forget. The realities of his existence are the shrewish aunt with whom he lives; his bestial and miserly employer; and his cousin whom he loves, but who, being only a schoolgirl in short dresses, is unresponsive to his passion. For his imaginary world he chooses a nearby château which he has never entered but which has always haunted his dreams. Supposing himself to be employed there as a servant, he pictures its weird inhabitants as a cruel and haughty young viscountess; her aged father dying of cancer; her half-demented brother, likewise tormented by the fear of death; and Death itself, vaguely incarnated in a ghoulish housekeeper. The feverish dreamer writes these visions in his journal, until its abrupt termination at the point where the viscountess, unexpectedly entering the young man's bedroom, suddenly locks the door behind her, and blows out the light—the moment in every amorous scene where Green always drops the curtain. The narrative is resumed at a later period by the young girl whom he loves and who relates her cousin's sudden collapse and death during a walk with her in the neighborhood of the real château. The people who actually figure in this unfortunate young man's life are quite as fantastic as the fictitious creations of his dreams. The aunt, who, though cruel to everyone else, makes a fetish of all sick people and would have loved her dead husband more had he been unhealthy, who despises her daughter because she enjoys good health, is as improbable as the imaginary viscountess with her brusque and unaccountable fits of silent laughter, her aimless barefoot wanderings through the night, and her brooding curiosity as she spies upon her dying father's agony. In other words, a nightmare atmosphere is maintained throughout. If, in this agonizing fifth in a series of lugubrious novels, Green has again proved himself a master, the reader's surprise proceeds not so much from the choice of subject matter in any single book, as from the fact that any writer should be content to reign in such an exclusively morbid domain.

The contemplation of so much suffering would be a greater emotional experience were it not apparent that for most of it Julien Green and not life itself is responsible. The failure of these ill-starred destinies to move us more deeply is due to our realization that though fate may be cruel, it is not so immutably perverse. Green has no desire to arouse sympathy for his characters; his ambition is rather to make us say: "How true, how real that is!" but he has a far greater chance of capturing our pity than gaining our credulity. His weakness as a psychologist lies in not having masked his own sinister intentions in the cataclysms he lets loose. It is his own ruthless hand which adds the touch of salt to every wound; which shoves these luckless people over their tragic precipice. Like Zola before him, he resembles a scientist injecting a helpless specimen with malignant bacteria in order to study the disease thus artificially induced. The poison once in circulation, Green gives a magnificent demonstration of its deadly course; but the fact remains that all this had to be concocted in a laboratory, and no amount of skilful chemistry can make of it the stuff of life. More applicable to Green is Pierre Lièvre's criticism of André Gide: "The author has only observed his characters' extravagant, anomalous side, without taking into consideration that only by supplying the rest of their personality would this extravagance or this anomaly be rendered human. What we seem to have, therefore, is the portrayal of a disease made independently of the victim."

And yet, so great is Green's talent, that we forget at times the test tubes. The landscape seems so trustworthy, small wonder if we are thrown off our guard. For in the creation of his pictorial background he has adhered with the strictest fidelity to truth. Able to vivify his stories with descriptive minutiæ of almost uncanny accuracy, he has obviously documented himself from actual localities. Indeed, no one since Balzac has so successfully conveyed the immured and stifling atmosphere of the provinces, that colorless existence where it would be revolutionary to pick the geraniums on Friday when one always picked them Saturday; to go for a walk at ten in the morning, when five in the afternoon was the usual hour. How doubt the reality of characters in this almost photographic setting? When we can hear the opening of every shutter around them, the creak of every chair? Nothing but the severest shock will waken our suspicions as to the unsubstantiality of this world. Unfortunately, it is Green himself who administers these shocks.

The greatest tax on the imagination is that any people, even in the most remote provincial town, could lead such isolated, antisocial lives. His characters are represented as without friends or social contacts, and although at times they bemoan their solitude, they apparently cannot alter this state of affairs. Their restricted life simplifies the author's task considerably, and in Adrienne's case—arbitrarily cut off as she is from all the friendships usually allotted to a young and beautiful girl—permits the apparition of a total stranger to produce such a catastrophic effect. Green allows her to meet only one man, and automatically he becomes the one she never should have met. Naturally, people so removed from their fellow-men will be ignorant of the world and of themselves; naturally, in their seclusion they will become the prey to dangerous obsessions and develop abnormal natures. Least of all are they permitted to love or be loved within the four walls of their homes, for Green may be called the destroyer of the legend of family love. Even his characters pause at times to marvel at their misery, and interrupt the narrative with frequent, if rather self-conscious, lamentations such as: "Never before have I felt so sad," or "To suffer more than I have today would be impossible," or like Adrienne, who, passing the night in a strange hotel, scribbles on a piece of paper: "Here at Montfort, the 11th of June, 1908, I have been more unhappy than has ever been the lot of anyone before."

The spirit behind Green's writing is strikingly akin to that of the painter Goya, who, having a marked preference for horrible scenes, used to decorate his walls with the more gruesome of his pictures: men buried alive, and monsters gorged with human flesh. Green too is attracted by the sight of human misery, and writes: "People always feel more at home in places where they have greatly suffered." Conscious of only malice and cruelty, he places a cancerous soul in every character he paints. When he presents a restaurant proprietress seated peacefully among her clients, he distorts her otherwise placid features by tracing in her eyes a gleam of demoniac curiosity. When it is a woman watching over her sick nephew's bed, he stresses the atrocious satisfaction she experiences at the young man's plight. Who but Goya could so dramatically evoke a murderer in a coalyard and flood the scene with moonlight? And just as in the case of the Spanish painter, the works of Green, with the possible exception of *Epaves,* are stamped forever on the mind.

If with *Adrienne Mesurat* Green had been content with one success in macabre vein, if he had not decided to assume permanently the rôle of bugaboo, perhaps the world would never have suspected that he was himself the bugabooed and that his own social adjustment was at fault. Undoubtedly one of the most sincere of men, he is at the same time the most diffident, and this clash of honesty and timidity may account for much of the implausibility of his writings. Shrinking from every social contact, trembling with terror when confronted by his fellow-man, he reduces to the barest minimum his first-hand knowledge of the world, an initial handicap for which no amount of talent and imagination—and Green has both—can entirely compensate. However, it would be unjust to accuse him of wilfully distorting fact. Just as dreamers never doubt the reality of their nightmares, Green in his panicky flight from his fellow-creatures would be the last to suspect that he was falsifying them in his books. Whether or not his creations are true to life, they are true to what he thinks of life. Since it is evident that he accomplishes, and beautifully, what he sets out to do, we are at a loss whether to censure him for his curtailed vision, or to praise him for his skill as a maleficent conjurer.

Henry de Montherlant

"EVERY adolescent writes a book," says one French critic, "but hides it away, ashamed of its immaturity." Montherlant, a grown man, not only continued to write such books, but to publish them. Swept from the schoolroom into the trenches, he had all too little youth, or rather, had nothing but youth. He became one of the "eternal young men" engendered by the war. These were caught young and released in very much the same stage of immaturity; they are eternal because their violent and abnormal initiation into life distorted and fixed forever their perspective. Far from being ashamed of his youth, Montherlant exulted in it. He believed that the most intelligent years are between the ages of twelve and seventeen, and in truth Montherlant's mentality remained for a long time at just about these levels. It is because he had not time to become a conformed and adult thinker that post-war literature was rejuvenated by this fresh, almost incredibly naïve mind.

It is moreover doubtful if he had any desire to become a thinker. He had only to look about him to see the sad plight of the intellectuals. This was the aftermath of the War, when conditions bred uneasiness of mind and disordered thinking. To Montherlant, many of the literary pretensions of his contemporaries seemed pure hypocrisy. According to his own account, he never knew the meaning of anxiety, so he decided to become the champion of the natural and sound minded as opposed to the effete and neurasthenic. If, judged by an intellectual standard,

Montherlant was not a brilliant figure, he yet commanded attention through his buoyant personality. So different from the majority, he had only to express an opinion to provoke a storm of protest. In return, his fighting spirit adopted an air of bravado. He resembled an insulted schoolboy "sassing" his pedantic superiors, and many of his preposterous, exaggerated statements are clearly traceable to this defiant attitude.

In his formative period he was greatly influenced by Barrès, who taught him to develop his personality at any cost. Montherlant had always liked to beat a drum, and he thumped out the *culte du moi* with unremitting vigor. Well born, rich, carefully educated, and of an iron constitution, he lacked nothing to foster his self-confidence. Never had an aristocrat been more convinced of his superiority, nor more disdainful of the rest of mankind. He reserved all his enthusiasm for his own activities. He himself drew up the list. "Nothing is simpler for me than to indicate precisely the great phases, at once superficial and profound, through which my life has passed. First, a Catholic symphony composed of various strains; my education in a religious college, the authors of ancient Rome, and the influence of Spain where I imbibed the spirit of the bullfight. The second was war. The third was sport." In reality, these were only variations on one unifying theme: disciplinary action, which was Montherlant's sincere, if sole, philosophy.

His birthday fell on the 21st of April. As this was also the anniversary of the founding of Rome by the She-Wolf's sons, Montherlant regarded it as more than a mere coincidence: he believed that the stars shaped his destiny. Was he not born of the race of the Roman twins, therefore ordained to be the guardian of Roman traditions? Adopting the Tiber as a symbol for the classical spirit, and the river Oronte for the languid spell of Eastern culture, he believed that the Roman waters should be purified of all contaminating Romantic inflow. "Two philoso-

phies have struggled for supremacy. The one, feminine in its
genius, is based on the unverifiable. . . . Its tendency is to
neglect the body. Of Oriental origin, it engendered Utopia,
which begot disorder. Alexandrianism, Byzantinism, Protes-
tantism, revolution, Romanticism, Humanitarianism, Bolshe-
vism, such is its progeny. On its seal is engraved a heart. The
other philosophy, virile, rational, and founded on nature, fosters
order and stability. It attained its most complete form in ancient
Rome after the conquest of Greece. It inspired Roman Catholicism, the Renaissance, tradition, authority, Classicism, nationalism. All modern ills can be reduced to the gradual diminution in
the last fifteen hundred years of the Roman influence in religion, politics, and jurisprudence, of the Hellenic in the arts and
sciences. France reached the lowest point in this curve when
Græco-Roman culture was officially renounced between the years
1900 and 1910. Since then, a reaction has set in." And Montherlant wished to play an active rôle; to cultivate in his own
life the sturdy virtues of the Tiber as opposed to those of the
flaccid Oronte. Classical civilization became his inspiration. As
a child his favorite study was Roman history, and when only ten
years old he wrote a life of Scipio Africanus. It was to the Rome
of the Horaces that he turned, for this was synonymous with
strength, constancy, and grandeur. Fascinated by her disciplined
soldiers, her games and splendid athletes, he strove to make of
himself a sort of *civis romanus*. That is why in his own life he
avoided the debilitating effects of mysticism, love, and revery,
and welcomed war, athletics, and bullfighting. His love of
antiquity even became the bond which held him a Catholic, for
he looked upon the Church not only as a second mother of
Roman civilization, but as the continuation of the Roman Empire
in the modern world. Since everything that happened to Montherlant, whether it be a spiritual crisis or the development of
his biceps, was deemed suitable material for a book, his novels

revealed his special interest of the moment, and marked his highly original reactions to religion, war, sports, and love.

His first novel, *Le Songe* (1922), recounts the extraordinary behavior of Alban de Bricoule (alias Henry de Montherlant) at the front. This young megalomaniac believes himself a sort of superman or demigod. With disarming simplicity he states: "Everything that is great I feel to be my father; it must be remembered that I am different from other men, and therefore not to be judged according to their laws." Not patriotism, but a craving for preëminence prompts him to enlist for active service in the trenches, for it is there that he hopes to experience "a dipping into the elementary," "a purification of the intelligence and heart." Welcoming death if accomplished in a burst of personal glory, he rushes to meet the exploding shell. A revolver at his belt (although he is only a simple private), a volume of Plutarch in his knapsack—for Alban is described as being more familiar with the ancient world than with his own—a bronze Gorgon in his helmet, this young Humanist warrior delights to fancy himself playing Caesar in a Roman army. War is a form of entertainment devised especially for him; the killing of his first German is the moment of his greatest exhilaration, and makes him rejoice in an institution which legalizes assassination. "It is natural that those killed by others should set your nerves on edge, but the most hideous corpse becomes a thing of beauty when it is you who are the killer." Alban's nearest approach to a tender sentiment is his affection for his former schoolmate Prinet, now his companion in the trenches, although even when it is a question of his friend, Alban's nature, fundamentally aloof, suppresses any display of emotion. At Prinet's death, however, he suddenly becomes a prey to abject fear, and loses further interest in his military career. To the reader, baffled by this sudden change of heart, Montherlant explains that most human conduct is determined by the need to love.

However, he differentiates sharply between physical desire and love, emotions which he believes can never be inspired by the same person. That is why two women figure in Alban's life: his mistress Douce, and Dominique, his platonic friend. Montherlant is never attracted by the charms of romantic love; indeed, woman is man's enemy in breeding weakness and disorder, qualities of the Oronte. The young athlete Peyrony, in a later book, is made to express Montherlant's own attitude of Roman misogyny: "A wife would be a hindrance in my sports. Look at the athletes who get married; their form deteriorates, they are finished." If the toreador hero of *Les Bestiaires* imagines himself in love with a young Spanish beauty, it is only because of the old tradition linking gallantry with bullfighting. Since feminine charm inveigles man into desiring that which at heart he despises, Montherlant looks upon love as a catastrophe: "The necessity of having to attract and repulse almost in the same gesture, to light the flame only to cast it away, as with a match, that is the tragedy of man's relationships with woman." Alban admires Dominique precisely because she is a young athlete whom he met at the stadium and whom he therefore believed immune from sexual desire. When later she reveals herself as an ordinary woman susceptible to temptations of the flesh, no longer able to respect her, he abandons her forever. Montherlant's specialty was to exalt fraternal love, and although in *Le Songe* fewer pages are devoted to Prinet than to Dominique, it is this fallen comrade who fills the hero's mind and heart.

Montherlant is apparently the only French writer who enjoyed the experiences of 1914–1918. He says: "France has her recent war to thank for coming into existence; we only made fun of her before." For him, the Armistice sounded the death knell of four glorious, active years. It was peace to which he could not adapt himself, for this meant devitalization. By a natural transition, he turned from war to sports for the theme of his next two books, *Le Paradis à l'ombre des épées* and *Les Onze devant la porte dorée* (1924). "Sports," he writes, "continued in my life that realism of war, which is one of the eternal and distinguishing features of the Tiber. If at the age of twenty-six I am a member of a football team, I am hearkening to the same voices which, sixteen years before, made me compose a life of Scipio Africanus." As a modern Pindar, Montherlant was inspired not so much by a love of athletics as by his need to counteract inertia, the aftermath of war. "The men who fought in the war for four or five years came home exhausted. They are a sacrificed generation. But people of my age, who only got in at the end, and besides were very young, brought back from the trenches a muscular tension which that life awakened in them and did not release. Perhaps they threw themselves into sport hoping thus to bridge the gap between the great physical lyricism of war and the bureaucracy of peace." Aiming to cure the soul through the body, Montherlant believed that just as cowardice and weakness breed vices, systematic physical training fosters obedience, loyalty, and many other neglected wartime virtues. So in *Les Olympiques,* we see him taking himself very seriously as a football captain, or as a runner in a stadium, where by exhorting his men to cultivate an idealistic attitude towards sports, he feels that he is equipping them for the greater struggle —life. He begins with his own body, which he puts in perfect working order. Indeed, his ecstatic contemplation of his own physical perfection, whether it be a shoulder blade or thigh, becomes amusingly Narcissan. In like manner, he devotes ten pages to the minute description of Dominique's muscles, and as many more to those of his friend Peyrony.

"Without ceasing to be Roman, I became 'taurine.'" Bullfighting is the theme of his next novel, *Les Bestiaires* (1926), which recounts an earlier period in Alban's life, when as a lad of sixteen he went to Spain to become an amateur toreador.

Montherlant had the same experience, and at the end of *Les Bestiaires* he cites with boyish pride extracts from various newspapers concerning his own exploits in the *corrida*. The 21st of April, the date of Alban's birthday as well as Montherlant's, not only commemorates the founding of Rome; it also marks the period when the sun enters the zodiacal constellation of the Bull. This made Montherlant and his hero feel that they were preordained to become priests of tauromachy. Imagining himself in love with Soledad, a beautiful but haughty young Spanish girl who has stirred his vanity, Alban extracts from her the promise of a rendezvous on condition that he first kill the most vicious of her father's drove of bulls. In spite of his inexperience and at the price of a painful goring, the youthful matador kills the bull, but is so revolted at the heartlessness of Soledad's cruel demand that he loses all further interest in her.

If Montherlant had been content to write a diverting and dramatic story of bullfighting, his book would have been more popular in France, but he insisted on idealizing the dubious virtues of this sport. He traces at length the history of the divine cult of the bull, from its ancient origin in the time of Mithras to its association in later centuries with the church of Spain. It is conceivable that primitive races should deify the bull, but when a grown-up Frenchman of today professed to believe in man's regeneration through the shedding of taurine blood, the sole effect on his countrymen was ironic laughter. Montherlant had read Barrès' *Du sang, de la volupté et de la mort,* and he took this to mean that war and the shedding of blood are akin to love. Did not Mithras bear the sword of the Ram, which was the symbol of Mars, and was he not carried by the Bull, the symbol of Venus? Alban declares himself too much in love with these bulls not to wish to kill them; only possession could satisfy his craving, and in the case of the bull, possession is fulfilled through slaying, symbol of the sacramental sacrifice. If deep within him lay the need for creative slaughter, he would have been equally willing to offer his own life as a tribute to the bull. For after death, was it not conceivable that he might be changed into a bull? Colette probably had *Les Bestiaires* in mind when she said: "I am thinking of espousing sometime an enormous cat; Montherlant will doubtless be glad to hear of this!" From his earliest writings on, Montherlant always made a point of expressing his scorn and antipathy for the human race. His instinct is to caress the bull, but he says he has never been able to see a man on the edge of a river bank without immediately experiencing a strong desire to push him into the water. However, it must be added that Montherlant also says he would fish his victim out again with the same enthusiasm.

There is an unpleasant sting of truth in many of Montherlant's accusations against the opponents of bullfighting. "I distrust people who are too fond of animals," says the Spanish duke in *Les Bestiaires*. "Probably they are wasting on animals a love which they do not feel for the human race. When they talk to me of an old maid who shelters dogs and cats, I am almost sure that she harbors in her innermost being a distinct hatred for her fellow creatures." Ernest Hemingway, whose *Death in the Afternoon* is said to have been directly inspired by *Les Bestiaires,* expresses much the same opinion: "I believe, after experience and observation, that those people who identify themselves with animals, that is, the almost professional lover of dogs and other beasts, are capable of greater cruelty to human beings than those who do not identify themselves readily with animals."

Montherlant points out that there was never so much talk of tenderness in France as during the Revolution, when torrents of human blood were shed. "And what party in Spain today finds the slaughter of the bullfights such a scandal? That party which incites in every possible way one half of the country to butcher the other half. These people have nothing against the shedding

of blood when it occurs in a civil war. They protest on behalf of
the horses in the ring, but they would be glad if all who dis-
agree with them were down there in that ring and under the
horses' hoofs." And to support his theory, he quotes a passage
from *Harper's Magazine:* "What! Go to a bullfight?" says an
American to an Englishman who has invited him to the arena.
"Never! If you'd promise me I'd see a man killed, I'd go with
the greatest pleasure. But don't ask me to see poor, defenseless
horses cut to pieces." And as to the wounded horses, Montherlant argues that it is only because of their size that they excite
our pity; if they were no larger than an insect, nobody would
mind their sufferings, just as no pity is felt for flies in their slow,
agonizing death on fly-paper. The only people Montherlant
suffers to protest against bullfighting are those who also protest
against hunting, fishing, the use of cab horses, the caging of
birds, the wearing of furs, the eating of fish or meat, and who
will not even kill vermin on their body. All others, he thinks,
should "hold their tongues, for their attacks against bullfighting
are either for political ends or are due to nerves."

Les Bestiaires marked a turning point in Montherlant's career;
and in *Aux Fontaines du désir,* written just one year later, he
revealed himself as a disillusioned pessimist. It was hardly to be
expected that war, sports, and bullfighting should prove very
substantial spiritual food. They temporarily assuaged his hunger
for grandeur, but in plunging him into a life of sensations they
awakened in him other more dangerous tastes. In Montherlant's
case, the god of hedonism proved to be a selfish, jealous deity,
which soon succeeded in overthrowing all his earlier idols. Not
that most of these had rested on very steady pedestals. Certainly
religion had never been one of his serious preoccupations. From
the time when Alban, confessed by the army chaplain at the
front, replies: "Sin no more? Ask of me something more useful
to God," and is absolved through the writing of three Latin

psalms, it is evident that Jehovah and Montherlant are on very easy-going terms. Becoming increasingly patronizing and derisive in his attitude towards the Deity, Montherlant finally disclaimed all religious faith and was proud of it. "One would have to be sorely tried," he writes, "to be reduced to accepting Jesus Christ. Not having called upon him when I was in desperate straits, it is most agreeable to be able to thank him now, for thanking people who have never done anything for you is always a pleasant sensation."

Nor had Montherlant ever been known to express a patriotic or humanitarian sentiment. "There is no need of leaving behind one a great work," he says, "no need of great intellect or heart. It is equally foolish to die for humanity or one's country, for these will eventually become as obsolete as God. Since there is no idea or soul which is worth the saving, all efforts in these directions are little more than madness." In *Les Bestiaires,* on the rare occasions when he mentions his countrymen at all, it is to point out their inferiority to the Spaniards. "In a Frenchman, vanity takes the place of pride. He will lick peoples' boots, but be ashamed to let a motor pass him on the road, fearful as he is of being compromised in the eyes of his friends. A Spaniard, on the other hand, has genuine pride, and is therefore a real lover of humanity." So the Frenchmen Montherlant selects to figure in his Spanish scenes are poverty-stricken men with unpolished shoes and dandruff on their collars. His own dearest wish was to be taken for a Spaniard, and Fate had sufficiently tantalized him by permitting him to be of partially Spanish ancestry.

If in Spain, which confuses its religious and its carnal thrills, and mingles God with bullfights, Montherlant chose the most natural of all countries for his experiments in sensual mysticism, he also hit upon the one beset with the greatest pitfalls. Barrès had been the first to direct his attention towards the fusion of sensuality in religion. But where the author of *Du sang, de la volupté et de la mort* was merely striving to teach that the spiritual could be attained through the natural, and the eternal through the human, Montherlant, with his more active nature, proposed to put these theories into practice. "You, Barrès, were content to remain on the sidelines of life and merely gaze on war, religion, and love. But I should never be satisfied with what takes place only in the brain. Blood? Death? Why you, Barrès, would faint at the sight of a bullfight. Voluptuous pleasure? Something whispers in my ear that you have never known it." This difference in their natures accounts for Montherlant's decision to forsake his former master, or rather, to surpass him. So, suggesting that an Angelus bell be placed in every stadium, and a chapel attached to the arena, he invited God to watch him at his football and applaud his exploits in the ring. In short, he only valued religion as a voluptuous ingredient in the wine of life, and writes: "If I were a thousand leagues removed from every thought of sensual pleasure, I should only have to enter a Spanish cathedral to be instantly assailed by carnal desire."

But it was characteristic of Montherlant either to go too far or not far enough with anything. Having tried and found wanting the Tiber, Barrès, war, religion, and sports, he abandoned one by one his early enthusiasms, even Spain. Accusing Barrès of having falsely praised this country, in his later books Montherlant concentrates on the obscene and repellent aspects of Spanish life. Sensual gratification alone remained. "Long live the senses!" he cries in *La Petite Infante de Castille*. "They at least do not deceive! I have never passed from the act of physical indulgence to the act of understanding without the conviction of having passed from wisdom to folly. When I enjoy the body, I possess reality, whereas through the intellect I should only arrive at some solution which tomorrow would be wiped out by another." He thinks that the modern man either no longer knows how or no longer dares to enjoy sensual pleasure free of remorse or literary trappings. Jeering at the type of person who invents all manner of religious and philosophical reasons for suppressing his innocent desires, Montherlant believes that indulgence of the senses is the most natural of all functions, and when no harm is done, should never be considered unlawful. "So much the worse for art if such a truth impoverishes it. I pity anyone who calmly accepts the thesis that the catechism adds piquancy to novels. Many authors, to be sure, would lack subject matter if deprived of a little evil here and there. But 'sin' and 'the devil'! What fuss about such exploded legends! Gide [and Montherlant might have included Mauriac] understands only that state of mind which is tormented by a sense of guilt. I find it impossible to conceive, much less admire, a troubled conscience in face of sex." His complaint is that when he himself proposed to live a voluptuous life and be frank about it, his experiences were termed puerile.

With Montherlant, however, self-indulgence soon assumed the proportions of an obsession, and this rocket which, ignited in the trenches, had sped through a stadium and an arena, finally exploded in a cloud of gross licentiousness, and fell to the ground cold and extinguished. Scouring Spain, Italy, and northern Africa in his inexhaustible quest for new sensations, he soon arrived at a stage of complete lassitude, when the only moments of real satisfaction and relief were his rare days of abstention. Vitiated by his excesses, he eventually found his sole pleasure in fleeing from pleasure. *La Petite Infante de Castille* (1929) is the story of one of these flights. Once again in Spain, he relates his experiences with a young Spanish dancer who attracted him by her innocence and beauty. He abandons the bewildered girl just as she has accepted his advances, because he prefers to the gratification of his desire the purely cerebral satisfaction of renunciation. For if Montherlant, a victim of his liberty and weary of himself, is no longer able to enjoy the realization of a dream, he still cultivates desire, and this, he says, is a pleasure infinitely greater than fulfillment. The obstacles he must sur-mount before arriving at "the gates of paradise" give him a sense of being alive and distinguish him from what he calls "the onanists of poetry," who are satisfied with merely dreaming.

It is not surprising that such a nature should have alienated the sympathies of almost every faction. There were, first, the Catholics, baffled as they were by a man who took the Sun-God more seriously than Christ. Nor could they forgive these pagan hymns in praise of sensuous living, these lapses into the most flagrant impiety. A man for whom the words 'sin' and 're-morse' had no meaning, must be a serious menace to the Church.

The nationalists were likewise irritated. Montherlant's rever-ent attitude towards bullfighting, so distinctly a Spanish institu-tion, did not endear him to these bulwarks of the state. The added drop of acid was his dogged praise of those qualities in the Spanish character which were conspicuously absent in the French.

The sentimentalists also felt abused. This group was not pre-pared to refute the annoying accusation that the world measures guilt according to the size and importance of the victim. How cope with a man who argued that the bullfighter is no more cruel than the pleasure-seeking fisherman who leaves his catch to die upon the shore? Nor could their code be stretched to include a soldier who openly rejoiced in the killing of a human being. As far as they could discover, the only occasion on which Monther-lant had been known to weep was in sympathy with a woman athlete who had lost her race.

But the intellectuals were the most numerous and, perhaps, the most wry-faced group. These older critics were men of sedentary lives, and their tastes were artistic or psychological. Everything in their training led them to look with scorn on all forms of brute force, and they could hardly be expected to welcome a young writer who idealized the body and extolled the natural, purely physical life. They had become so unaccustomed to romantic lyricism of any sort that enthusiasm for such a juvenile occupation as sport seemed perfect rot. This attitude is especially prevalent in France, where the intelligentsia have an instinctive distrust of the athlete with his unwarranted vanity. Montherlant, in turn, found their hair-splitting distinctions ridiculous, and mocked the psychological type of mind which attaches importance to the things he deemed insignificant. So there ensued a lively warfare, in which Montherlant was denounced as a presumptuous adolescent, and his critics as untidy old fossils.

However, there were many critics who admired just those traits for which Montherlant had been so severely censured. Under his audacity and extravagant parade, they discovered moral courage and nobility of soul. Pointing to his earlier impassioned *La Relève du matin* and *Le Songe,* they called his recent demoralization and lowering of standards the temporary pose of a nature fundamentally mystic and pure. If they disagreed on the quality of his artistic gifts, they approved at least of his evolution from the turgid lyricism of his early books to the greater precision and directness of his later style. Montherlant's Spain is a gorgeously colored canvas where blue skies, yellow buttercups, and shimmering fountains give brilliant relief to the sinister blacks and reds of the bulls and bleeding horses. He has painted haunting pictures of the World War—notably, the impenetrable nights and even more desolate dawns of No Man's Land. In his unusual way Montherlant was also a psychologist, and his admirable analysis of emotion, whether it be the athlete's anguish in the drama of the race, or the matador's cold fear before the ordeal in the ring, revealed him, if not an intellectual giant, at least as an artist whose virile originality deserved recognition. As Montherlant's heroes bore a striking resemblance to himself, they possessed snap and personality. A few moments with Alban de Bricoule will stamp him forever on your memory: "O God, if Thou wilt grant that Prinet be still alive, I make this solemn vow: I swear to forego during a long period, three years perhaps, all exercise of my intelligence; I promise not to read a single book, nor to express myself in literature; should a thought come into my mind, I will resist the temptation to jot it down, and will leave my mind completely uncultivated." From a passage such as this, it can perhaps be seen why Montherlant should exasperate certain readers and be the delight of others.

A few years ago, it seemed that the past tense was to become associated with his name. At the age of thirty-eight, burning all letters and photographs, he decided to forsake his home and countrymen, and start life afresh in another continent. After his meteoric literary flight of ten short years, he declared, from a hiding-place in northern Africa, that he would never write again. Fortunately this decision was not immutable, and Montherlant has reappeared. Whatever part the enigmatic African civilization played in the rekindling of his energy, he emerged, with his recent realistic novel, *Les Célibataires,* an infinitely greater artist. Under a pseudonym, it would have been difficult to detect the new Montherlant who, abandoning his former juvenile interests, now chronicles with studied objectivity the dismal lives of an uncle and his nephew, two pusillanimous noblemen, whom their poverty obliges to live together. If the impulsive, headstrong youth is dead in Montherlant, not so the misanthrope to whom this study of decayed aristocracy offers a vast field of grim enjoyment. It is another delightful opportunity to push overboard the man on the river bank, and if we are to believe his word, his two dirty, lazy, self-pitying, egotistical, cowardly 'celibates' are not worth the saving.

To prove his point, he selects the two most abject and futile bachelors his irate imagination could evoke, and with merciless scalpel dissects their withered lives. "Imagine in the society of today," he writes, "this monstrosity: a man without employment but likewise devoid of all ambition; a poor man, uninterested in money." Heaping every insult on his ignominious pair, branding them as sexless imbeciles and unkempt *débris,* he constantly emerges from the wings to ask such questions as: "Reader, can't you see that there is some flaw in the machinery which gives impulsion to such lives?" In describing the ill will lurking in this family group, he caustically concludes: If a man has one drop of meanness in his make-up, he invariably reserves it for his aged father or his mother. It was meanness, he avers, that kept the old Count de Coëtquidan alive, for "meanness, like alcohol, preserves. After a certain age, each biting word that you pronounce, each slander spread, makes you gain a few months over the grave, because your vitality is stimulated. This is to be seen in animals, when a particularly cruel hen or an ill-tempered dog lives longer than the others." Indeed, M. de Coëtquidan had subscribed to a newspaper in the country merely to force the postman to walk some sixteen kilometers daily to deliver it. Hardly more attractive is the young Count de Coantré, who avoided amorous adventure; first, because his linen was never fresh, and secondly, because he had no real desire. Or the wealthy Count Octave, so mean that "his face became transfixed and almost spiritualized whenever he thought he had duped his fellow-men"—upon which Montherlant comments: "The same sentiment can be detected in the kennel, where the most intelligent dogs are always the most vicious." More than a splenetic description of two bloodless and effete old men, Montherlant's book is a bitter satire on France in general. As he casts his eyes about contemporary Paris, he discerns, in the ugly neglect of both man and matter, a lack of pride which enrages and disgusts him. He cannot pardon his era for its "great confusion of values," which he calls the devouring and uncleansed wound of modern society.

With the aristocrat singing to the tune of "Stupidity of the Social World," the *bourgeois* to that of "Honor to Manual Labor," he deplores the modern masochism which makes each class undervalue and calumniate itself.

But it would be quite beside the point to seek a moral, even a warning note, in Montherlant. He is too indifferent to his fellow-man to have the slightest thought of guiding him. "Here are," he seems to say, "two miserable and repulsive men. Take them or leave them, it's all the same to me." However, the world of letters will both take and pay homage to his sordid celibates, for they reveal that a vehement younger writer has found a new and effective vehicle, and that the great school of French realism may survive in the most unexpected quarters.

Pierre Drieu La Rochelle

WHEN in the early chaotic years which followed the World War Drieu La Rochelle first took stock of his country in *Mesure de la France* and other political essays, he was regarded as one of the most intrepid and promising leaders of his generation. Those were the days when ex-soldiers felt they had earned the right to voice their opinions. As their self-appointed spokesman, Drieu proclaimed: "We of the younger generation are of a grandeur unknown to our forbears. It is now our turn to speak, that of the older men to keep silent. We scornfully turn our backs upon those sad prophets who were as doubtful of themselves as they were of us. In times to come, the world will talk not of our defeated fathers, but of us, the descendants of this obscure lineage. We have made history, which is a very different matter from merely having read it." It was a gratifying discovery for many of these new post-war writers that the world was disposed to take them so seriously. Undeterred by lack of experience, they rushed into print. Not the least fanatic, though obviously sincere and conscientious, was Drieu, one of those recalcitrant spirits whom the baffled critics were glad to dispose of by calling them "Princes of Youth." Some of these princes, later reduced to mere commoners, were forced to capitulate to life and assume more chastened tones. In the course of his career as fustigating political reformer and novelist of manners, Drieu has become less arrogant in his attacks, but he has never cried defeat. He has faltered and groped, to be sure, when his guiding star grew dim. But the feverish pilgrim stumbled on, and he has finally reached a haven.

If, according to the contention of some psychologists, it is only the unhappy, thwarted nature who seeks refuge in creative art, Drieu La Rochelle is another soul in pain who found relief in literary expression. Unfortunately the degree of pain is not the gauge of inspiration, and Drieu's is not a brilliant talent. He himself admits that he has no natural gifts, and in his autobiographical novel, *Le Jeune Européen,* he confesses it was because he gradually found himself without money, friends, children, and a vocation that he first turned to writing. Begging his public's indulgence for having embraced a literary career, he asks: "What was left but to become a writer if only to bid farewell to the human forms which one by one were disappearing over my horizon?" However, it was more than through cowardice and to earn his daily bread that Drieu became a man of letters. Idealistic and patriotic, he is fundamentally a moralist and a disciplinarian, whose instinct is to preach and reprimand. Drieu's characteristic note is acerbity and ill humor, which, without the saving grace of genius, makes him a dreary and forbidding writer. Of all the men presented in this brief survey, Drieu is the one least apt to be known or enjoyed by the American public. A worthy bore, he must be reckoned with, for however chilling his attributes, Drieu demands recognition as a representative figure in contemporary French thought.

His first books, so many wails of complaint and dissatisfaction, reveal him as a Jeremiah, militant through his tears. He was a fault-finder from his earliest years, at least in retrospect, for it cannot be supposed that children are so hypercritical. His first *boutade* is *Etat-Civil* (1921), an autobiographical essay recounting his childhood and adolescence. In this series of monotonous and humorless pictures, in which he prescribes for his elders' shortcomings with the same zeal he devotes to his own grievances, the only period spared the long-suffering reader is the author's infancy between the years of one and three—too early, Drieu laments, to be recalled. Born of affluent, over-solicitous parents, he was brought up "in cotton-wool and the fear of draughts." He reproaches first his mother, for allowing him to remain an only child, for abandoning him too much as a little boy, and later guarding him too much a prisoner at her side. Having pilloried his father and his grandparents on various scores, he even reviles the family furniture which, being of the department-store variety, lacked soul and was symbolic of the human slaves who manufactured it. He next rebukes his early teachers, old men "in whose veins flowed the meager sap of city trees" and who seemed bent on exterminating the last vestiges of childhood lingering in their unlucky pupils. Nor does Paris escape the universal ban, "that epitome of rottenness, senility, stagnation, and solitude," whose Sorbonne is "paltry and anonymous, new as a suburban *Hôtel de Ville,* open to every noxious fume and thronged with neglected adolescents soiled by their coarse puberty."

In the spotlight before this anathematized background stands the child Pierre, by no means too prepossessing a figure himself. To follow his own description: "An instinctive distrust, a determination contracted before my birth, made me rebel against everything my mother offered me. I remember that as early as my seventh year, every time I walked with her, I took virulent delight in thwarting all her kindness and in poisoning that day's happiness for her." Scarcely more appealing is Drieu the schoolboy, whose popularity must have been sadly impaired by his mania for meddling in his playmates' lives. "I had a passion for the public good. I wanted to see everyone around me bathed in a harmony pleasing to my soul. Forcing my comrades into what I considered paths to paradise, I experienced a profound emotion in imposing my religious ideas on them." To render the

youthful zealot justice, it must be added that Drieu was also
prepared to toil and suffer for his friends, provided that in return
he was duly admired.

Drieu was twenty-one years old at the outbreak of the War.
He had just completed his military service, to which he was to
add four years of active service at the front. It was in the full
flush of his youthful exaltation as a soldier, in 1915, that he
wrote *Interrogations,* a little volume of free verse which glorifies
war and its ally, death. Distrustful, like Montherlant and other
belligerent spirits, of the enervating effects of peace, he writes:
"I sing of the War because it is inseparably linked with
grandeur. The War for men like me, born as we were in a long
period of peace, was a fulfillment of our youth which the
younger generation hailed with joy. Introducing into our lives
a solemnity which human events no longer seemed to promise,
it should never be looked upon as a catastrophe. And peace?
Pacifists, what is your peace? Is man to end his days as a retired
shopkeeper?" Obsessed by dreams of power, believing that
might makes right, a partisan of 'sword-intelligence,' Drieu
found the Germans a congenial race: "O Germans, I have
never hated you! You have strength, the mother of all good!"

Against his own country, on the other hand, he directed the
bitterest of philippics. There can be no doubt that at this period
France was the greatest passion of his life. "I love her," he
writes, "like a woman one follows in the streets. She is disturbing and fascinating like all chance encounters. I can also say
that I love my countrymen, even when they are brutes, cowards,
gluttons. Not because of a certain genius which may be theirs,
but because they are the men with whom I've lived. If only for
the privilege of making obscene jokes and of discussing women,
I would willingly follow them into another planet." But Drieu's
nature was that of the reformer who chastises what he most
deeply loves. He thought France had sinned and deserved to be

admonished. The more he berated her, the more he betrayed his ardent nationalism. His idol had toppled into the dust and must be kicked back upon the pedestal.

Having grown up in a period when France was still smarting under the Franco-Prussian War, Drieu added to the mortification felt by every Frenchman at this recent humiliation an exaggerated consciousness of his country's defeats throughout the centuries. He asserts that as a child he suffered acutely at the thought of disasters as remote as those of Crécy, Poitiers, and Agincourt. Hence his love of France was ever associated with pain. "Parents, why did you not keep silent on my country's ignominy? I was ill from France's illness, and everything around me reminded me of her insignificance in comparison with Great Britain, Russia, and the United States."

This is the theme of his political essay, *Mesure de la France* (1922), where in an alternating barrage of statistics and grandiloquence he draws up specific charges against his countrymen and prescribes panaceas for their ailments, whether these be flabby muscles or race suicide. "France held her head too high in this war. But her bloodless body would have been unable to sustain the weight had not the strength of twenty nations been added to her limbs. We French cannot claim to have been the sole possessors of this mistress Victory." And hurling his oft-repeated invective against his country for her sterility, he adds: "Unlike the Germans, our fathers were unwilling to have children, which is our crime. We tempted a proud and self-sufficient people, and by cynically displaying our weakness, invoked their scorn and hatred. France, ardent and dried-up mother, it is time for you to investigate the condition of your belly and your brains!" His lamentations pursue their lengthy course through the ills of capitalism and the various manifestations of modern materialism. Believing that money has become the universal god, he asserts that all classes of society have been reduced to the same level in a civilization of business men bent solely on gain. "Men of today are devoid of all passion, and share in common their system's resultant vices of alcoholism, inversion, and onanism. Does Lenin in his Kremlin differ from a Stinnes or a Schwab? What the world needs is a moral, intellectual, and political reintegration—not a revolution but a new birth."

This was also the conclusion of the hero in *Le Jeune Européen* (1927), easily recognized as Drieu, in spite of willful autobiographical disparities. The story concerns the career of a young dilettante of twenty-one, who after having dissipated his vitality in polo, skiing, hunting, and bejeweled adventuresses, having roamed to the four corners of Europe, "that great toy I should have liked to smash," finally yearns for a world upheaval to relieve the monotony of life. Suddenly at Deauville, in August 1914, his Hispano overturns, and this is coincident with the declaration of the World War: the playboy is metamorphosed into a trench-digger. "I had already exhausted motor racing, cocaine, and Alpinism; in this stripped and desolate Champagne I found the sinister sport I had so long been sensing in the air. Just as childbearing is the woman's mission, men are made for war."

Being a man of action, his hero enjoys the carnage. Moreover, being formed in Drieu's youthful image, he experiences his highest flights of mysticism in the midst of this human butchery. A victim of contradictory impulses, torn between the need to dream and the need to act, Drieu had once declared: "Along the misty shores of revery, I have lost all desire for life; languid but happy in my lethargic state, I should like to perpetuate a nocturnal navigation on the river of eternal bed-sheets." This theme, a recurring *motif* in the chaotic architecture of Drieu's life, throws light on much of the anomaly of his nature. It is responsible for the cigarette case he is said to possess, on which is pictured the meeting between Goethe and Napoleon. It accounts for the Young European in the trenches when, deprived of worldly pleasure, he feeds his famished soul on Pascal. However, after a few months' contact with the monotonous reality of No Man's Land, Drieu's hero tires of both blood and prayer, and longs for something new. Deserting from the army, he arrives in America, only to become a prey to fresh disillusions. Drawn into what he calls America's national occupation of dollars and cents, he finds life in the New World as arduous as it had been at the front. He toils in an office, only to emerge at dusk into a labyrinth of narrow streets which, gorged with human flesh, remind him of the trenches: "The skyscrapers seemed no higher than the trajectories of our guns, and all this mass of humanity resembled soldiers hurling themselves forward to the assault of impregnable strongholds, as if in obedience to an absurd command dictated by an anonymous telephone. Americans cannonade nature; Europeans, deceived by ancient customs, fire upon each other. But let peace come, the world reverts only too eagerly to canned goods and cheap automobiles." Indeed, in the American, according to Drieu, may be recognized the worst type of European, who has only changed continents in order to play more easily the game of dollars. "The Americans are the oldest race I know; they are senile. In flocking to Europe, they are merely satisfying their nostalgia for the old. More advanced than we in their industrial evolution, further removed from the mysteries of nature, they are fifty years of age while we are only forty."

For those readers who are weary of battling with the political situation; who have long ago despaired of rehabilitating Europe, and realize their helplessness in face of either capitalism or communism; who hate dilemmas and the necessity of choosing between Moscow and Geneva; who refuse to become athletes or parents of numerous offspring, there remains a Drieu who, when he turns from public affairs to the study of social types, writes in

a lighter, though always castigating, vein. By no means finished
with problems, he has selected an insoluble one. The people he
holds up to satire in his novels are thoroughly sophisticated men
and women who have deliberately chosen the type of life they
wish to lead. They are at once the fashioners and the victims of
the corrupt society in which they move. Drieu places them in
drawing-rooms, lends them a pseudo-cultured vocabulary, passes
them as members of the smart set, and then says, Look at these
awful things. Through this vitiated background of libertines,
nymphomaniacs, drug addicts, and inverts, slips one central
figure, for whom Drieu in a moment of inspiration found the
name of "the empty suitcase." He sticks this label on only one
of his heroes (*La Valise vide* in the four short stories comprising
his *Plainte contre l'inconnu*), but the epithet applies equally to
all the others, as they bear a striking family resemblance
(*L'homme couvert de femmes; Feu Follet; Drôle de Voyage,*
and others).

In *Le Jeune Européen,* where Drieu traces his literary career,
is explained the origin of this *valise vide.* "When I finally
decided to write of someone other than myself, I started to look
around among my friends. Selecting the most conspicuous person I knew, a man called Jacques, I asked him to look at me
fixedly for a moment. Then gazing obliquely at him through
my spectacles, I was amazed to find him covered with a thousand little blemishes, as though he had suddenly contracted a
skin disease, so that I accused him of having deceived me until
that day. From this misunderstanding was born the heavy and
lifeless caricature which I entitled the *valise vide* and which
had no little success, since people always like a portrait in which
they recognize the model."

From the character of Gonzague, we learn that the 'empty
suitcase' is a good-looking young man of twenty-two with the
intelligence of a child of ten. Smartly dressed to the point of

foppery, well mannered, alternately communicative or strangely
reticent in regard to love-affairs which never seem to materialize,
he is in comparatively straitened circumstances and, unable to
persist in any occupation, in constant need of loans. An habitué
of bars and resorts of frivolous entertainment, a collector of
matchboxes, uniform buttons, and a thousand other baubles,
he has never been known to read a book, attend a concert, or
visit a picture gallery. He craves affection, but lacks the vitality,
constancy, or emotional depth to attract either friendship or
love. However, rather than be left to his own devices, he will
attach himself to anyone. In short, he is an empty piece of
luggage who creates an infectious emptiness around him. Drieu
renders his hero's situation all the more pathetic by not entirely
depriving him of nobler instincts, but he depicts him as so
debauched that these instincts, far from constituting a regenerating force, merely serve to destroy his gratification in the sensual
life he has no thought of renouncing.

Drieu's second 'suitcase' is even more dilapidated. The hero
of *L'homme couvert de femmes* has become so effete through
erotic dissipation that he is no longer capable of experiencing
love, his one obsession. Seeking the soul of a virgin in the body
of a prostitute, he finds it impossible to enjoy the possession
of either without evoking the image of the other absent one.
Since in Drieu's books the woman of the salon has all the earmarks of the woman of the streets, it is difficult to understand
the hero's hesitation between the two. Indeed, he does not hesi-
tate but rushes with alarming rapidity from one to the other,
the prostitute being the more difficult to acquire as she demands
money. And so, the 'man covered with women' is doomed to
remain forever unappeased in his search for 'esthetic concupiscence.' Like the earlier *valise vide*, he aspires to higher things
and secretly yearns to experience paternity. In the creation of a
child, which he calls "the symbol of the physical union and

tangible token of love's reality," he sees man's one opportunity "to participate in the divine mystery of life." Love without issue, on the other hand, he regards as little short of onanism. Deciding that solitude is his only refuge, he finally turns his back on brothel and boudoir. The book ends before he has had time to return to either.

The hero of *Le Feu Follet* is equally libertine and equally deprived of love. Being a man of greater action than either of the previous empty bags, he resorts to drugs and eventually to suicide. "If I kill myself," he says, "it is because I am not a successful beast. It is also because literature and the world of thinkers have wounded me with their abominable lies. Though they know full well that sincerity is impossible, they persist in talking of it."

A later novel, *Drôle de voyage,* is a semi-sardonic, semi-lugubrious version of the old story of Panurge. As in Rabelais' satire, the hero is alternately motivated by his desire to marry and his fear of the consequent loss of his liberty. Gille Gambier, this latest of Drieu's men of many women, is visiting for economy's sake at the country estate of some rich Jews. To quote a monologue: "It is true that I am thirty-five and for a fortnight have been living here in complete seclusion. I am not spending a cent, and at my forty-fifth year, when I shall no longer be attractive to women, the two hundred thousand francs which I have kept intact will provide for me. I shall remain a bachelor, forever separated from women, all of whom at heart are bourgeois. Whole days have passed since I have touched a human body. But I am so saturated with flesh that all I need is to close my eyes and—oh! what a relief, this close of day! It is the hour when great pipe organs melt, annul, and confound the vitality of life." Drieu's specialty is to write novels on love in which nobody loves, and, whether intentionally or not, the conversation never rises above a certain smartness. Perpetually philosophizing and generalizing, Gille, caustic but less penetrating perhaps than Drieu imagines him, concludes: "Women love nothing. Least of all do they love love. That is reserved for men. Women do nothing, are nothing. Even in the choice of their jewels and clothing they depend on men." Or again: "At bottom, girls and women are alike. Unmarried girls are unwilling to have too good a time because they wish to secure a husband; married women are just as unwilling to enjoy themselves because they wish to keep their husbands." When not only the hero, but each member of this rich and futile milieu joins in such reflections as: "Madame, you must resign yourself to seeing your daughter marry an attractive man who will be unfaithful to her, or an unattractive one to whom she will be unfaithful," the reader is apt to lose sight of the satiric import of the novel, to flounder aimlessly in its mire of tarnished epigram and cheap cynicism.

When the story is permitted to pursue its dismal course, we learn that Gille, haunted by the bitter sense of loneliness, has decided to punctuate his dreary life by marrying some innocent young girl. Beatrix, an English heiress, is at hand, to whom, after several days of half-hearted philandering, he finally considers himself engaged. When Beatrix departs for her home in Granada, Gille, morbidly depressed during his fiancée's temporary absence, engages in a liaison with a married woman in Paris. Thwarted in his efforts to inspire or experience love in this illicit union, he retreats to Spain to rejoin the ever hopeful Beatrix. No sooner arrived, however, than he plans to abandon her once more, alarmed as he is by her unsophistication and lack of voluptuous beauty. So he resumes his weary quest of that nonexistent woman who will satisfy at once his senses and his heart. *Drôle de voyage,* perhaps Drieu's masterpiece, is not without successful moments. Take this realistic picture of the desolate young couple: "Beatrix dragged her fiancé around the

Spanish countryside: an old young man, long with an even longer face, a sort of imitation Englishman, imitation diplomat, imitation brother, who had no craving for her breasts or lips, who found her shoulders too thin, her face too dead, and whose least desire was to take in his her emaciated fingers." Gille's tragedy, like that of the average Drieu hero, is a fundamental inability to reach the heart of any woman, for his heart shrouded by morose egotism, his mind corroded by cynicism, and his intellect benumbed by laziness, condemn him to perpetual frustration. In short, the *valise vide,* Drieu's one original contribution as a portraitist, points a warning finger to the mental, moral, and emotional impotence of modern man.

Unlike his early peremptory strictures, when Drieu delineates this highly specialized social type, he speaks in tones of despairing pity rather than of blame. This was a milieu which he himself frequented, and he asks that no hatred or venom be detected in his portraits. This request cannot be granted for his recent collection of war stories, where his inherent bitterness crops up once more. There is the first one, for instance, *La Comédie de Charleroi,* with its portrait of the war mother, who with pretentious vulgarity exploits her son's heroic death at the front to enhance her own prestige. Of excellent workmanship, these latest stories of Drieu reveal maturing skill, although Drieu has yet to prove himself a master story-teller.

An exasperated patriot and a nauseated spectator of society, Drieu is less a man of letters than a dynamic force. In 1924, when Drieu was first appearing on the horizon, one farsighted critic, Crémieux, prophesied for him a long career, but queried whether it should be one of literature or politics. Indeed, during the period when he was devoting himself almost exclusively to the *valise vide,* Drieu seemed to have lost all interest in public affairs to whirl in a frenzied social vortex. People wondered whether his "curiosity towards life, his fatalism, coquetry, obliging compliance, lassitude, and sense of justice," instead of leaving his repulsion intact, might finally cause him to dissipate his vitality, or perhaps flourish in this corrupt atmosphere. His recent conversion to fascism seems the reply to all these queries. If for years his pent-up energy found outlet only in fitful spurts of rage and spleen, a mine of strength was fermenting underneath, and that this wounded idealist should gravitate towards the rigid discipline of fascism was inevitable and fore-ordained. A logical entrenchment for the humorless man of action, it was the one and perfect answer to his lifelong quest.

Jules Romains

Few writers have experienced a more triumphant comeback than the sturdy Jules Romains. Many readers had become a little weary of the visionary poet of *La Vie unanime,* the expounder of paroptic vision of *La Vision extra-rétinienne,* the technical innovator of *Le petit traité de versification,* the cult-founder of *Le Manuel de déification,* the Rabelaisian mystifier of *Les Copains,* the hoax-lover of *Knock* and *Donogoo-Tonka,* the mystic communist of *Cromedeyre-le-vieil,* the meticulous psychologist of *Lucienne,* the sensual fetishist of *Le Dieu des corps,* and the exponent of telepathy of *Quand le navire.* He was a man of so many interests, or rather, he so merged his interests, that it is not strange if he failed of complete success in any one. As a student he had specialized in biology, mathematics, and philosophy. It was only by a narrow margin that he decided to become a writer of fiction rather than a scientist or a sociologist. For many years a professor of philosophy, Romains never entirely succeeded in thrusting the blackboard from his life and, with chalk and pointer in hand, turned everything he wrote into theorems in support of his ideas. Many of his readers disliked this spirit of *quod erat demonstrandum* and thought the dogmatic professor spoiled the poet. Nor did the average novel reader feel comfortable in this chill atmosphere of scientific objectivity. Lucien Dubech, always prompt with a caustic word, called him "a man not too intelligent, but one too exclusively intelligent." Obviously, Romains in his early period was a writer who did not entirely satisfy.

It was only in 1932, with the publication of the first volumes of his serial novel, *Les Hommes de bonne volonté,* that Romains transformed all complaints into salvos of applause. Calling his earlier books mere preliminary experiments for the forging of suitable implements, he offers at the age of forty-seven a work which brilliantly vindicates this long period of preparation. But *Les Hommes de bonne volonté* is more than a supreme demonstration of his particular theories, more even than superlatively good novel writing. As a rich and microscopic mirror of its century, it will probably rank in importance with such social documents as *La Comédie humaine, Les Rougon-Macquart* and *A la recherche du temps perdu.* More than the mere novelist of the hour, Romains may survive as the most important writer of his era, and, if we are to believe his critics, the first quarter of the twentieth century will belong as much to Romains as a similar epoch, a hundred years earlier, belongs to Balzac. True prophecy or not, Romains' unfinished masterpiece has already been pronounced in both Europe and America one of the most important events in the history of contemporary literature.

It is with heightened interest, therefore, that the world turns back to examine Romains' earlier works. These reveal an extraordinary correlation. If, before his final triumph in *Les Hommes de bonne volonté,* Romains diversified his art by five books of verse, five one-act plays, five comedies, five tragedies, five novels, and—alas, for the mathematical symmetry—four books of tales and essays, he unified his interests through one insistent theme. Probably no writer has adhered with more unswerving fidelity to a central idea.

He stumbled on it in his eighteenth year during an evening stroll through Paris. He was in the Rue d'Amsterdam, a populous quarter, and Louis Farigoule, later to be known as Jules Romains, was in a receptive frame of mind. This virile young pedestrian was primed for deep emotions. His parents, of hardy peasant stock, had endowed him with a robust constitution. His mind, equally sturdy, was richly nurtured on the sciences and the classics. His native home in the Cévennes mountains was a region famous for its spirit of rebellious independence. Romains' rebellion was against Catholicism, and he became an agnostic. "The world should have seen in me," he writes, "a young man whom religion had unsettled and made ill, just as later I was to become unsettled and rendered ill by war." But his was a nature which would not submit long to torment. If he had passed through a crisis of religious doubt, he still remained a poet and a mystic in search of a new God. "How glad one would be to have a God," he muses a few years later. "What loving words we should find to say to him." However, Romains insists that it must be a simple God of the streets, and not an abstract divinity of the clouds. "Ideas and ideals disgust me. I want a being. We want gods and we will have them. But gods whose flesh we can touch and who will be ourselves. Humanity is God."

Although Romains had lived in Paris since this early childhood, when his father had come to Montmartre to teach school, the city streets were still a source of wonder. On this memorable walk, he gazed with intense curiosity at every vehicle, shop, and passer-by, feeling suddenly that all these individual rhythms were part of a larger pulse of life. So his heart went out to the manifold activities of the street, to which he ascribed collective consciousness, or, as he called it, soul. Being in a crowd, he asked himself whether the individual or the crowd was the principal reality. The crowd was obviously the stronger of the two, and Romains concluded that the only entity was the group. Thus was born his famous theory of *unanimisme* which, sprouting from Paris sidewalks, was to haunt his imagination all his life.

Convinced that *unanimisme,* although primarily a poetic impulse, could be put to practical use, and made to modify the trend of modern life, he felt the importance of his discovery. His succeeding walks were fraught with new significance. Ecstatically alert to the city's slightest cry or movement, he would immerse himself in the streets for hours on end, "able to differentiate, with closed eyes, the sounds of one street-crossing from another, and to receive from the ground, the walls, the sky, a thousand communications which I treasured in my heart." These experiences he believed endowed him with mediumistic lucidity. Such sociologists as Durkheim, Le Bon, and Tarde had already expounded, among other principles of *unanimisme,* the psychology of the crowd; poets such as Whitman had sung of it; but Romains insists that he read these works at a later period and arrived at his own conclusions by paths of "pure intuition, mystical ecstasy, and love."

Imparting his new beliefs to a few chosen friends, in particular to the poet Chennevière, who possessed a love for humanity similar to his own, Romains induced his *copains* to join him in his wanderings. Comradeship, indeed, is one of the fundamental tenets of *unanimisme.* In order to identify themselves more closely with the populace, this small band would disguise themselves as workmen and apaches. If their spirit was democratic and fraternal, it was also disorderly, and they startled these humble quarters with many a prank and brawl. Admitted a short time later to the Ecole Normale, Romains indulged still further his taste for practical jokes and became one of the most intrepid ringleaders of the unruly Normaliens.

Feeling his way and crystallizing his ideas in a few early poems (*La Ville consciente; La Conscience de la ville; L'Ame des hommes*), and, while still at the Ecole, in a longer volume of verse, *La Vie unanime,* Romains finally launched a manifesto of his creed, which he called a *Manuel de déification* (1910). This sensational title was apparently misconstrued, for critics spoke of Romains' inordinate pride as the would-be founder of a new religion of which he was at once the high priest and the god. Romains' only claim to being an innovator was that he had been the first to direct the world's attention to eternal psychic forces hitherto lying idle. In fact, he never speaks in terms of 'I' but always 'we,' and suggests: "If anyone has doubts about *unanimisme,* let him create it for himself." Essentially a religion for the lonely soul, it is addressed, according to his manual, "to those who have lost all desire, but are too lazy to do away with themselves; to those who come home from work with lowered head and heavy shoulders and find each evening as sorrowful as the night before; to those who are rich but bored; to those who are poor and full of bitterness." It was because of his own loneliness as an individual that Romains sought refuge in the crowd which, if it submerged his personality, also lent him its strength. Believing in man's right to be happy, he writes: "We should not permit our soul to be ill. If the old moral system frightens it, let us abolish it. We may lose the Christian's paradise thereby, but our fusion with the mysterious forces of the universal destiny will more than compensate our loss." And so, in *La Vie unanime,* the youthful poet, bored and weak when isolated, forgets his personal ideas and beliefs in the joyful pulse of humanity. The French, always markedly individualistic, looked askance at a philosophy which deified the crowd. Would not *unanimisme,* they asked, mark the defeat of personal life, or worse, prepare the way for triumphant communism? But if Romains urged a concentric rather than an egocentric attitude towards life, he was seeking not the annihilation of the individual, but his enrichment through participation in the warmer feelings fostered by the group.

Having thus early thrown in his lot with *unanimisme*— Romains was only twenty-five at the writing of his *Manuel*— he made of each succeeding work a vehicle to develop and illustrate its principles. Although many of his tales make fascinating reading aside from their didactic import, the ultimate enthusiasm for Romains' art will be gauged by what is thought of *unanimisme*. Some people have no desire to vibrate in unison with the crowd; they studiously avoid parades, mass meetings, and athletic stadiums. Naturally, this type will be antagonistic to a doctrine which glorifies trains and army barracks. In *Les Puissances de Paris,* analyzing the synthetic soul of a great metropolis such as Paris, Romains renders homage to the various aspects of its collective life: its streets, squares, busses, excursion boats, amusement halls, and libraries. Any instrument of human communication assumes importance in his eyes, and his attitude towards telegraph wires, paving stones, and doors savors of reverence. Who but Romains would be so inspired by railroad tracks as to write: "Like gilded hair, all these rails took flight, and ascended towards a point in the black heavens where the stars were faintly showing. These golden threads were so perfectly stretched, they converged in so beautiful a movement, that the eye seemed inadequate to grasp their harmony. This almost required another sense; and perhaps a purer perception would have been able to hear music rising from all these nocturnal chords." Describing, in *La Mort de quelqu'un,* an old man's journey from a country village to Paris, first by stagecoach, then by train, he minutely records the commonplace vicissitudes of public transportation and the simultaneous sensations these produce upon such a heterogeneous group of travelers as a peasant, a shopkeeper, a schoolmaster's wife, and a wine-merchant: the solidarity and family feeling engendered by their hours of forced companionship; their common impatience at delays; and their unanimous impulsion towards the machine which is carrying them to their destination. But group consciousness as conceived by Romains is capable of a subtler sensibility, and in portraying a small and insignificant funeral cortège as it winds through the streets of Paris, he ascribes to these humble pedestrians "a consciousness of their unimpressiveness, from which they experienced a feeling of relief. Yet they had scruples about admitting to themselves this humble pleasure, for this would have looked too much like resignation."

Since Romains believes that the group itself is a blind unit dependent on the leader's sight, the quality of its collective vision will be determined by the powerful personality or dominating idea directing it. In *Le Bourg régénéré,* a short 'legend' in prose and the first of Romains' experiments, the initial impulse happens to be good. It springs from no more romantic source than an inscription scribbled in the public urinal of a small and drowsy town. More through caprice than a desire to educate, a post-office employe had written: "He who possesses lives at the expense of him who works; whoever fails to produce the equivalent of what he consumes is a social parasite"; and these words, originally embodying an alien idea, slowly ferment in the minds of the various citizens who read them, until, reacting logically according to their intelligence and caste, they ultimately arrive at the unanimous conclusion that their city must be modernized.

In *La Mort de quelqu'un,* the regenerating influence proceeds from the death of an obscure Parisian mechanic, a 'nobody' who had hitherto passed unnoticed, but who by the simple act of dying fires the imagination of his humble neighbors and unites them in a common interest. The pride of the *concierge,* who is the first to discover the corpse, the summoning of the aged father from the country, the buying of the mortuary wreath, the ceremony of the funeral: these emotions are commonplace enough, yet they suffice to inspire in these simple-minded people a sense of fraternity and a vague preoccupation with death. Romains wishes to show man's interdependence, and how the most universal and commonplace experience may have a far-reaching effect. It is a poetic version of the theory of protoplasmic survival, for did not the humble workman really live until that hour when his memory became completely effaced?

Selecting in *Les Copains* a small band of seven friends, men whose congeniality of temperament and tastes had made them sufficient unto themselves, Romains shows how a smaller group may impose its wishes on the crowd. A glass of wine too much completes the inebriation of the 'pals,' and they embark on an adventure. Deciding at random on two obscure provincial towns, Ambert and Issoire, they propose to descend upon these peaceful communities and shake them out of their lethargy. Through various tricks they succeeded at Ambert in addressing the un-suspecting citizens from the pulpit and transform a church serv-ice into an orgy of concupiscence. At Issoire, at the unveiling of a monument, the statue suddenly comes to life, and the town is thrown into a panic. A masterpiece of rowdy humor, this is a book for men, and not too squeamish ones at that. Indeed, we are not only first introduced to the *copains,* we take leave of them, in a state of disorderly intoxication. But what has become of *unanimisme?* Perhaps Romains thought he was becoming too serious in his presentation, and deemed it time to introduce a lighter element. "When it becomes impossible to deify a group," he writes, "make it laugh instead." But what is fun for the perpetrators of a joke is not so humorous for the victims, forced as they were at Ambert and Issoire to face social revolu-tion, not to mention the undue increase in birth rate. Humor is one of the constituent elements of *unanimisme*—"people isolate themselves to weep, but they unite to laugh"—and there are critics who discover a constructive force in the chuckles of the *copains.* However, it is difficult to find edification in this ribald form of caricature. If it is there at all, it lies in the joyous friendship of these seven men.

If it were not for the recollection of Romains' student days and his own delight in playing tricks, we might suppose him to be writing in defense of the crowd, generally represented by him as gullible and easily led astray. Is not the author secretly in league with his hero Knock, as this quack inoculates a hitherto healthy community with an exaggerated disease-consciousness? (*Knock.*) Does Romains seriously advocate such a group consciousness as animated the inhabitants of Cromedeyre-le-vieil, where a stubborn, proud, and self-sufficient people become so communistic that they build their houses opening into one another, construct their church from their own rock and forest, choose their priest from their own ranks, and create their own god, but where, on the other hand, the citizens become so oblivious to the rights of others that, needing to supply their one deficiency—women—they abduct the girls from a neighboring town? (*Cromedeyre-le-vieil.*)

At all events, the World War intervened, and Romains' early enthusiasm for group movements is said to have cooled. He saw the tragic imbecilities perpetrated by nations. Attributing the blame not to any single country, but to collective stupidity, he cries out in his war poems: "Europe, I will not permit you to die in this delirium! Cling on, brace yourself, crush the terrible god!"

However, he had no thought of abandoning *unanimisme*. Having described the unanimous effects of such abstractions as Death and Friendship, he next experiments with Love. He believes that the union of a married couple, joined by the closest of physical and spiritual ties, is unanimous life in its most acute and highly concentrated form. This is the subject of his triptych novel *Psyché,* which, beginning with *Lucienne* in 1921, was carried on, some seven years later, by *Le Dieu des corps* and *Quand le navire*. Although *Lucienne* is independently interesting as a love story, it only takes the hero and the heroine to the threshold of their real adventure, which is their marriage, or, more particularly, the most thrilling episode of their married life; the husband's telepathic vision of his wife.

From the beginning, Romains' work has revealed his interest in psycho-physiological phenomena, and the soul-almost-visualized-in-space had become one of the familiar aspects of his creed. Since he regards the body as an intermediary between the outside world and the soul, he assigns a rôle of prime importance to the eyes, its most sensitive point of contact. According to his theory of paroptic vision (*La Vision extra-rétinienne*), the sense of sight is not confined to the retina of the eye, but all the body cells may be trained to see. Touching, modeling, caressing the space and atmosphere around him, he sees the world from a plastic point of view. He speaks of "the palpable thickness of shadow," "the solid padding of space," "tangible air which reigns within a room but separates you from it, producing a sensation of fulness, of cheerful crackling comparable to the bubbles in champagne." Believing that physical matter becomes transfused with psychic forces, that thoughts and sounds throng the air, he thinks it possible for places to become permeated with human electricity: hence his expression 'mental air.'

It is not surprising that in *Psyché* he should push this theory one step further, and reason that under the proper conditions, human beings can project themselves through space.

The heroine Lucienne is first seen as a young woman earning a modest living as a piano teacher in a small provincial town. For pupils, she has two sisters, Cécile and Marthe, each aspiring to marry their cousin Pierre, a naval officer, who pays them frequent visits. They are doomed to disappointment, for Pierre has almost instantly bestowed his affections on the newcomer, Lucienne, who reflects, accepts, and marries him.

At first glance, this would seem to be just another married couple. Pierre, positive and ironic by nature, is not given to romantic effusion. Nor is the reserved and analytical Lucienne a sentimental dreamer, although she has visions; her first being the premonition of Pierre's existence before she ever heard his name. Like Romains, she is endowed with extraordinarily acute perceptions, and is peculiarly sensitive to atmosphere and space; she is conscious of voices mounting vertically, thoughts forming circles, angles, lines; even the spacing of furniture in a room becomes mystically significant and reacts emotionally upon her.

Aided by these psychic propensities, Lucienne emerges rapidly from the somewhat arid, spinsterish young woman of her unmarried years into an ardent and voluptuous wife. For that Pierre is also responsible, being determined that their physical union shall remain a novelty rather than become a routine. Before the experiment, he had some misgivings as to the modest and unsophisticated Lucienne; he even speculated on her possibility as a lover. Her resourceful coöperation soon reassures him on this score; indeed, her zeal and aptitude surpass his fondest hopes. *Le Dieu des corps* is a most appropriate title, for this enthusiastic pair naïvely make of their sexual transports 'a religion,' and call their hours of intimacy 'the carnal kingdom,' whose throne is a bed. The French have always approached the sexual act with disarming simplicity; Romains deifies it. Anyone but Lucienne would squirm under the algebraic gaze of a husband like Pierre, who resolves her anatomy into an equation.

Permeated as she is with Pierre's love, Lucienne suffers a painful amputation when, a few months later, he is obliged to leave her to resume his duties as a purser. Since they both keep minute journals of their lives, we are informed of everything that happens during their weeks of separation, just as we had earlier been entertained with details of the wedding night. Lucienne, with her more delicate sensibility, is the greater sufferer, and if a union through space is to be effected, we surmise that the generating force will be the young wife's. This miracle Lucienne accomplishes by dint of almost superhuman concentration, and one night in his stateroom Pierre beholds the apparition of his wife through some 1,500 kilometers of intervening space. If Romains' readers are not so completely convinced as was the skeptical-minded Pierre; if the world is always annoyingly insistent on scientific confirmation, Romains at least gives an interesting turn to *unanimisme,* and pays homage to a new god, Love. *Unanimisme,* in fact, is primarily a religion of the senses, a sort of sensual pantheism: hence the unsympathetic conclusions of critics such as Rousseaux, who calls it "the consolation which the body can offer to a philosopher who has lost his soul."

But Romains had by no means lost his soul; or if he had, he redeemed it through his faith in man. And this had been growing steadily throughout a quarter of a century. Just as in each succeeding poem, drama, and novel, *unanimisme* had been growing warmer and more supple, less conspicuously labeled, so Romains, in conformity with his own precept, had, in unclenching his fists, been opening his arms, until with *Les Hommes de bonne volonté,* he reveals that he means to be a prophet of good will. With eight volumes already published, he has uncovered the lower stories of the colossal edifice he plans to build. Its dimensions are so vast, its objective so great, that we may well be astonished at the energy and ambition of its architect. Believing himself the exponent of an idea capable of rejuvenating society, enthusiastic as all proselytizers, he proposes to paint no less than an exhaustive panorama of contemporary

Paris and give an encyclopedic vision of modern man. Although conservative estimates place the final number of volumes at twenty, enthusiastic boosters anticipate many more. Romains himself, fearful of disheartening his readers from the start, refrains from giving figures; he only vouchsafes that his work will be very, very considerable, and a glance at the author's massive jaw convinces us that he will see it through. At all events, the gigantic monument proceeds with heartening modern speed, shooting upward, or spreading outward, with two volumes annually. All that the author demands of his public is patience, and—the keynote now of everything he says—good will. So he begs us not to turn back at the portico, but to suspend judgment until the completion of the roof.

Although he has only concentrated on this work for the last twelve years, he has meditated on it much longer. Having devoted his entire career to a study of psychical communication, he offers *Les Hommes de bonne volonté* as the culminating demonstration of the validity of his claims. If some of his former works, such as *La Mort de quelqu'un* and *Lucienne,* were already brilliant achievements, if many of his earlier building stones reappear in this larger structure, Romains is now quarrying from finer marble and has surpassed all previous undertakings. However, it must be conceded that the average reader's patience will be severely tested, for he stumbles into an incoherent labyrinth of individual adventures and tantalizing suspensions in the story. To assist our memory in this multitude of characters, presented independently of each other, the author supplies indices and short summaries of the plot, the only apparent link so far being the epoch in which these people live— six years before the World War; and the home they share in common—Paris. In fact, Romains warns us in his introduction not to expect a central character, for he says the time is past when it is possible to group modern life around an individual.

So he does not concentrate on the activities of a selected minority, but strives to evoke a composite vision of the whole. That is why he has constructed a vast revolving stage presenting rapid glimpses of workmen, soldiers, financiers, politicians, professors, literary critics, students, priests, secret service agents, anarchists, coachmen, prostitutes, housewives, countesses, a small boy with a hoop, without forgetting the sophisticated little mongrel dog, Macaire. In bewildering succession we witness incoming trains, race courses, the Bourse, the Métro, chimneys, kitchens, salons, boudoirs, brothels. In the aristocratic quarter live the de Saint-Papouls; in the fashionable, the Sammécauds; in the provincial, the de Champcenais; in the populous, the Bastides; in the Latin Quarter, the two students, Jerphanion and Jallez. A thief commits a murder; a book dealer becomes involved and in his turn kills the thief; an adolescent loses his virginity; a business man corners Paris real estate; a countess undergoes an abortion; a kept woman is worried about her sugar investments; an idealistic priest succors an abandoned woman; oil magnates pursue their shady schemes; the pros and cons of freemasonry are weighed; the Church is revealed in all its grandeur and defects. Honest men become corrupted; idealists learn to compromise; faithful wives become adulteresses: for these are never static snapshots, but reels of constantly changing life. For this mammoth and heterogeneous canvas, Romains has investigated every social milieu, conceived all possible combinations of events, probed all emotions. His characters are real because reflected from every facet: sexual, sentimental, intellectual, and spiritual. Conversations are reported literally and uncut; rooms are described even to the weave of the carpet, or their dimensions in feet and inches. We are supplied with the menus of every dinner, and the statistics of every business deal, artistic selection being the least of the compiler's preoccupations in this most garrulously courageous of modern encyclopedias. A few volumes of *Les Hommes de bonne volonté,* and we know how half of Paris sleeps, eats, dresses, thinks, works, schemes, hates, and loves.

The novel resembles an enormous toy racetrack where each horse is moved forward at unequal intervals. For in order to convey an impression of simultaneity of action, Romains usually allots a given character but one chapter at a time. Thus, in her opening scene, the actress Germaine Baader is introduced asleep in bed at nine in the morning. In the succeeding eight chapters, many new stories are set in motion, but in the ninth, Germaine is getting dressed. After two more intervening chapters she is lunching with her lover; four chapters more and she is watching Paris in the twilight. By the end of the first book, *Le 6 octobre,* which is a sort of symphonic overture, we have reviewed but a single day in her existence, just as we have read of the same day's experience in the lives of some fifteen other people. Occasionally, in the heat of his story-telling, or perhaps as a concession to the reader's curiosity, Romains devotes as many as four or five consecutive chapters to a single character, enough at least to warrant naming a book after him. This accounts for the title of the second novel in the series, *Le Crime de Quinette.* However, Quinette pays dearly for this unusual prominence, and in the next two volumes, *Les Amours enfantines* and *Eros de Paris,* he is only permitted a few paltry appearances, just enough to remind the audience that he still exists before a new and even longer exit. But so sharply cut are these characters' profiles, so original the rôles assigned to them, there is little danger of their being forgotten. It is Romains' art to stamp their images so indelibly that for long periods he can abandon them with impunity. Morever, it is never at the price of our credulity that he achieves such vivid pictures. If his characters are unforgettable, it is not because of their fantastic improbability, but because his situations, familiar enough in real life, have never before been utilized in fiction. Individually, a countess or a midwife might soon become effaced; but his countess negotiating with his midwife is a memory that endures. Romains is not the first to introduce us to an unromantic Babbitt, nor to stage a house of prostitution; but he is probably the first one to trace every movement of a practical-minded realtor when he enters one. It is due to countless episodes such as these that *Les Hommes de bonne volonté* is more than a richly checkered fresco; it is life itself.

Romains planned his first four books as a prologue. "The events in the individual lives which I depicted," he informs us, "were meant to hold less significance than the knowledge gained about these characters—their backgrounds and the common origin of their lives—from all of which is to spring the ulterior movement of the drama. My readers will have noticed that this first series of events extended over a very limited period of time, and that with twelve hundred pages I have only covered some three months of the year 1908. From now on, for a certain number of volumes, the pace and arrangement of the story will perceptibly change, and I shall follow more rapidly and consecutively certain actors and bring them once more to a new threshold in time, a new landing-place. However, I hope that this will not be accomplished at the expense of our losing a complex and many-sided view of things, nor the impression of their organic multiplicity, their incessant correlation, and their juncture." And so, having carefully built up the philosophical and sociological background of Paris in the early years of the twentieth century, Romains, in his next two volumes, *Les Superbes* and *Les Humbles* (1933), proceeds to trace somewhat broader lines. Even though he undertakes a more definite architectural configuration by concentrating, first on 'the haughty,' and then on 'the humble,' two opposing columns of society, it would be rash to conclude that Romains is planning to adhere to an obvious symmetry. Indeed, in the two latest instalments of his novel, *Recherche d'une église* and *Province* (1934), the line seems more obscure than ever. Deeply reflective books, they plunge us into new moods and expose the philosophical and political currents fermenting in Parisian life as the war of 1914 drew nearer. One of these was freemasonry, which Romains analyzes as one of the antidotes sought by men to relieve their mental solitude. Why, he wonders, should the citizen of modern Paris, whose life to all outward appearance seemed full to over-flowing, still seek the support of some creed shared in common? So he collects the intellectuals of all grades and ages, and seats them around the café tables in the Latin Quarter, where they discuss the question "Why are we so isolated?" This was Romains' golden moment to prove the miracle which *unanimisme* will perform. Hence his preoccupation with occult societies, religious factions, and political groups, which will continue, as they have always done, to modify the trend of history.

It is not to be supposed that all of Romains' race-horses will reach the goal simultaneously. Many will doubtless fall by the way, and perhaps only a chosen few will come in at the finish. If there is to be a final coördination of all these multitudinous organisms, this will be psychical rather than physical, since most of these characters will presumably never meet. Any blending of their lives will probably result not from chance encounters, but from deep psychological currents which will make brothers of them all. This will be accomplished by the ever simmering *unanimisme,* whose special manifestation, if we can believe the title, will consist in good will. To be sure, Romains has so far given us but few indications of its presence in the great vortex of modern Paris. As yet he has vouchsafed the barest minimum of pure altruists, and from these few obscure and unassuming men are shed the rather scant rays of charity and human sympathy in a universe otherwise depicted as devoid of spiritual warmth. Nor do the others seem to be suffering very keenly from their lack of idealism; indeed, Romains' specialty is to paint a cheerfully courageous, if all too self-centered, world. Where one of Julien Green's characters would complain: "Never before have I felt so miserable!" Jules Romains' exclaim: "How could I possibly be happier!" Their minds may be bent on selfish and material ends, but this does not prevent his men from whistling as they shave, nor his girls from feeling romantic as they powder their noses or comb their hair.

So the skeptics will ask whether Romains' 'men of good will' do not constitute too insignificant a minority in a world of covetous, egocentric men and women. Can a few sparks of nobility and human kindness scattered here and there kindle the crowd's inherent good will into an unanimous and mighty flame? "Yes, they can!" cry two Normal students, Jerphanion and Jallez, supposed to be Romains' mouthpiece and the Greek chorus of his drama. One is an alert, inquiring young man from the provinces; the other a Parisian seeking some rule of moral conduct apart from religious dogma, and sensitive like Romains to the emotional currents of the crowd. Together they constitute a portrait of the author in his youthful days, a composite of his idealistic and his intellectual nature. "One thing is certain," they conclude, as from the roof of their college they contemplate the mysterious Parisian maze beneath them. "Society is bound to change. The idea of justice is irresistible. A mere drop suffices, and from the day when the world accepts this drop, one can foresee that there will be no rest until everything has been made over and transfigured."

Gradually, cautiously, Romains has revealed an important secret, and one that separates him from the majority of modern thinkers: he has dared to be an optimist. Unlike those modern pessimists who retreat to an imaginary world in order to forget the injustices of life, Romains plunges joyfully into reality. Where some of his contemporaries, resorting to such anesthetics as dreams and the subconscious activities of the mind, remain expectantly still, Romains, advocating the active life, seeks to increase his contacts with the world. "I am not one of those who find a bitter gratification in the contemplation of ultimate incoherence. I am not addicted to the dilettantism of chaos and confusion. The world, no doubt, is anything you like to call it. But it is out of this dispersion, these zigzagging efforts and disorderly growth, that the ideal of an epoch ends by disentangling itself. Myriads of human activities are scattered in all directions by the indifferent forces of self-interest and passion, even of crime and madness; and they proceed either to destroy themselves in conflict or to lose themselves in the void. But of all their number, some few of these activities are endowed with a little constancy by the pure in heart, and this for reasons which seem to respond to some elementary design of the Spirit. Everything comes to pass as though the Whole had chosen to progress by a series of clumsy jolts. In this confusion of wills, there must surely be some of Good Will." And Romains believes that there is more of this than is readily apparent, or that men who possess it themselves realize. "Men of Good Will! May you some day once more be assembled by Good Tidings! May you find a sure means of recognizing one another, to the end that this world, of which you are the merit and the salt, may not perish!"

At present it seems futile to speculate as to what Romains' intentions are in all this good will. It may lead him to socialism, communism, or internationalism. Many readers believe that he is mustering his small army of characters only to plunge them headlong into the cataclysm of the World War. Since that was an epoch when the white race almost succeeded in annihilating itself, it will be curious to see what evidence in favor of good will he will extract from it. An easier task would be that of demonstrating not where good will, but the lack of it, has led. Or as one malicious critic has said: Is not the patient reader who trudges wearily through the interminable galleries of this monumental labyrinth, who must await the twentieth, perhaps the fortieth, volume of *Les Hommes de bonne volonté* to know whither he is being led, the Man of Good Will *par excellence?* But however blind may be his path, and however tiresome certain of its stretches, it leads through countless rich pastures, which when finally patched together will reveal that Romains has reconstructed an entire epoch in French history, with all its aspirations, impotence, and charm.

André Malraux

STRIKING the dark minor chords of revolution and death, André Malraux shatters any hope that the theme of Good Will is to remain the final harmony. His stories of suffering, fright, and self-annihilation are perhaps the harshest dissonances in contemporary French letters. Of all expedients resorted to by modern thinkers in their attempt to escape reality, Malraux's is the most defiant and heroic, for he proposes no less than the bitter anodyne of self-immolation. He refuses to subscribe to any flight at all, and if he denounces 'man's fate' and the vanity of existence, he thinks we should stand our ground and die. His heroes seem even eager to provoke catastrophe; they search for the path over which some Juggernaut will pass. The sacrifice is invariably ineffectual, but they have the grim satisfaction of causing a momentary lurch as the inexorable chariot passes over them.

Among many possible Juggernauts, Malraux's choice falls usually on China, for in his travels through the French protectorates he had early absorbed its fetid, suffocating atmosphere. Against this background he paints the universal drama of revolution. Social unrest and impending anarchy were particularly marked in the Far East. Invaded by foreign agents from every state in Europe, exploited by propagandists and unscrupulous profiteers, bristling with bolshevists and revolutionists of every sort, China had become the dog on which most of the political experiments of the Western World were tried out. The structure of the ancient Empire had proved so moldy that under the blast of occidental ideas it immediately crumbled into dust. Untroubled by inventions, discoveries, cares, desires, or worldly ambitions, China had slumbered for centuries behind her Great Wall. Everyone tried to differ as little as possible from his neighbor; each day contrived to resemble as closely as possible the preceding one. Its ancient creeds are well summed up by an aged Chinaman in one of Malraux's books: "It is good that such things as the total submission of women and the institution of concubines should exist. Women are subservient to men just as men are subservient to the state. Do we live for ourselves? We are nothing. We live only for the state and the order of the dead throughout the centuries." The sufferings of women under such a régime are expressed by one of the Chinese mothers he portrays. A young bride has just attempted suicide, and her mother exclaims: "Poor child! She nearly had the good fortune to die!" Nor were the thinkers or philosophers more reassuring: "My father," says one young man, "believes that the essence of life is anguish. Consciousness of one's fate gives birth to every fear, even that of death. Fortunately, opium serves to liberate, and therein lies its usefulness." A world founded on despair and lethargy was naturally doomed to perish. Rounds of machine-gun fire transformed China's traditional exotic sleep into a nightmare of anarchy, strikes, and civil war.

In 1911 the Kuomintang, originally a secret society, later the republican national party, had succeeded in overthrowing the Manchurian dynasty. Under the leadership of Sun Yat Sen it extended its activities to the south. After this agitator's death in 1925, it invaded the central empire. China finally became so emancipated and modernized that with the influx of the Russian soviets it seemed about to capitulate to communism. In 1927, the Kuomintang under General Chang Kai Shek shook itself free of the bolshevists, and communism was temporarily crushed. This was the politically turbulent China that Malraux knew and chose as the setting for two of his novels, *Les Conquérants* (1928), and *La Condition humaine* (1933). In *Les Conquérants,* the story of an insurrection against the British domination in Hongkong, we learn that the insurgent forces are composed of two factions: one includes the bolshevist leader and other professional revolutionists; the other is more disinterested, and like the hero Garine, is fighting for ideals. By birth a Swiss, educated·in France, Garine served in the Foreign Legion during the European War, but, disappointed in his hopes of an active life, soon deserted. Always attracted by revolution, he next threw in his lot with the bolshevists in Russia, only to be disillusioned again by what he calls this party's "doctrinal claptrap." Upon the invitation of a friend he came to China, where, entering the service of Sun Yat Sen, he worked himself up in the Kuomintang until, at the beginning of Malraux's story, he has become the director-in-chief of the revolutionary propaganda. When the Chinese are victorious against their oppressors, he is no longer interested, and if he does not first die of his malaria, he seems likely to instigate a counter-revolution.

Although there is no revolution in Malraux's next book, *La voie royale,* there are three rebels against society: Claude, a young Frenchman who, railing against "the vanity of a cancerous existence," is bound for Cambodia in search of archeological remains; Perken, his enigmatic traveling acquaintance; and Grabot, a fugitive from justice, who has escaped to the wilds of the Cambodian forest. As an example of human energy, Grabot has always fascinated Perken, who, now on the trail of his old friend, induces Claude to go with him, as they are bound by a similar hostility to all the petty manifestations of civilization. At the risk of their lives, they succeed in tearing from the jungle a few carved rocks, and proceed to track down Grabot, whom they finally discover, a prisoner, blinded and tortured in a remote

Cambodian village. The unfortunate man is rescued and avenged by the French troops; but, threatened by reprisals from the natives, Claude and Perken are obliged to abandon their loot, Perken eventually dying from an infected wound.

La Condition humaine, Malraux's third novel, is an infinitely richer and more complex work, although lacking the interest and unity of his two previous books. This time he relates the failure of the Soviet revolution in Shanghai. In the dramatic opening scene, the youthful terrorist Tchen plunges his knife into the sleeping body of a Kuomintang agent and steals the mandate authorizing the delivery of arms for the repression of the communists. Soon after this, Tchen, though tormented and haunted by his first crime, tries to assassinate General Chang Kai Shek by throwing a bomb at his passing automobile. The attempt fails, for the General does not happen to be in the car, and Tchen, horribly mutilated by the explosion, prefers death to capture, and fires a revolver into his mouth. Other conspirators are the intellectual idealist, Kyo Gisors, son of a Japanese mother and a former professor of sociology at the University of Pekin; the ironic but tender-hearted Russian nihilist Katow; the chimerical and grotesque Franco-Hungarian Baron de Clappique, gambler and antique dealer; the Belgian Hemmelrich, whose phonograph shop is their secret meeting place; and finally their chief, if invisible, leader, Malraux. The counter-revolution is represented by the cold-blooded and cynical French capitalist Ferral, president of the Franco-Asiatic corporation; by the brutal German König, chief of police; and by the much dreaded Chang Kai Shek advancing with the army of the Kuomintang. As a background for these cosmopolitan figures, mill and grovel the motley Chinese populace with its famished coolies, soldiers, workers, strikers, and prostitutes; with its evil-smelling streets, brothels, opium dens, and dance halls; its din of tongs, drums, bagpipes, and clattering wooden shoes. The insurrection is finally crushed and the revolutionists are condemned to be burned alive in a locomotive boiler. Thus Katow meets his death; Kyo, awaiting a similar fate, swallows poison; while Clappique and Hemmelrich, by means of a disguise, effect their escape.

A good deal of *Les Conquérants,* and even more of *La Condition humaine,* is as disorderly as the period described. Unable or unwilling to proceed by clear, straightforward narrative, Malraux unfolds his stories in a maze of short scenes, wireless messages, and heavy doses of statistics. It must be assumed that the average reader is less documented than Malraux on the complicated political situation in Indo-China. Serenely indifferent to the layman's ignorance, he lingers on munition reports and organization details instead of satisfying a natural curiosity in regard to the Chang Kai Sheks and the Tcheng Tioung Mings. Nor do Chinese names help us to differentiate between the Lings, Hings, Tongs, and Changs. These books are filled with flying bullets, barricaded streets, and bloody skirmishes, but just who, why, or where anyone is fighting is almost impossible to discover. The long passages of unclaimed dialogue do not clarify the situation. When not indulging in frequent philosophical aphorisms, his characters speak as if delivering military dispatches, a type of perfunctory conversation obviously introduced for explanatory purposes. When the reader expects to hear something about a speaker's personality, it is hard for him to become interested in a tank report. In this welter of characters, no single one receives sufficient attention from Malraux to engage our sympathies. These battle-scenes would be more thrilling if we cared who won. Since the scene of *La Voie royale* is the depths of a tropical forest, Malraux has less chance of befuddling his readers, but even in this sparsely populated area, there is a confusing array of fighting tribes. Thus, in spite of the fact that *La Condition humaine* won the Goncourt prize, many people find Malraux's book tedious to read.

Perhaps conscious of these defects, in his latest work, *Le Temps du mépris,* a long short story recently published in *La Nouvelle Revue Française,* Malraux very markedly tightens his narrative and concentrates on a short period in the life of a single character. This is the imprisonment of Kassel, a communist propagandist, in a Nazi jail, his ultimate release and reunion with his wife and child. So skilfully timeless are rendered the agonizing hours he has spent in this Inferno, that the reader shares the hero's stunned surprise on learning that what seemed an eternity has been but nine days. Indeed, his gruesome experiences are strangely out of life. Placing in beautiful symmetry the most divergent elements of human nature—on the one hand, harsh cruelty; on the other, stoic martyrdom for one's beliefs— Malraux liberates his hero from his prison only to make him plan how he may again court death. "And this was life again," are the words with which he hails his liberty, and we know that Kassel's destiny is to perish for his creed.

Except for this recent, if brief, demonstration, in *Le Temps du mépris,* of Malraux's skill in concentrated narration, his artistry has chiefly been revealed in the extraordinary strength and poignancy of individual scenes. Always alert to effects of light and shadow, he first calculates the illumination of his stage. An artist in black and white, he has a preference for prison or night scenes, mist and blinding sunshine. Since his characters are usually seen emerging through some slanting band of light before disappearing into the surrounding shroud of darkness, his most conspicuous stage accessories are swinging lamps, candles, electric signs, or lighthouse beacons. Relying on strongly contrasting lights, he accentuates the psychological note he wishes to strike. Drama is added to the meditation of one solitary old man, in *La Condition humaine,* by "the shadow of his finger running suddenly from the wall to the ceiling." And a touch of coarse strength to another character, seen for the first time in a brilliantly sunny room, where "the shadow of his heavy nose, cast on the whitewashed wall, made a dent in a Cambodian painting." It is probably due to Malraux's skill in chiaroscuro that the assassination scene in *La Condition humaine* stamps itself so vividly: a bedroom plunged in darkness whose only illumination comes from the neighboring building, "a great rectangle of pale electricity cut by the window-bars, one of which streaked the bed just below the sleeping man's protruding foot, as if to accentuate its volume and its life. Was this foot the extremity of a body? Tchen felt compelled to see the body; to see the head, and for that it would be necessary to enter the strip of light and let his squatty shadow fall upon the bed." The murderer's movements are then traced with all the deliberation of a slow motion film. Tchen removes the dagger from his pocket; raises it slightly in his right hand; glues his left hand to the woolen blanket; wonders whether the body will resist the dagger; tries piercing his own left arm with it; approaches the bed; yes, he has made no mistake in his man; the sleeper moves his foot; Tchen shudders; raises his arm, and—two pages later— strikes.

Other outstanding scenes in the same novel reveal the self-sacrificing Katow surrendering his precious cyanide of potassium to two fellow-prisoners, less courageous than he in face of the blazing death awaiting them; Hemmelrich returning to his shop to find his Chinese wife and young son mowed down by machine-gun fire; Ferral, furious at being jilted, revenging himself on his mistress by releasing in her room a kangaroo and $800 worth of birds; Kyo's young German wife May begging his permission to follow him into danger, "one tear gliding down her nose and remaining suspended on the corner of her mouth, where by its secret agitation, poignant as the pain of animals, it betrayed that the immovable death mask of her face was still alive." It is by the accumulative effect of such tragic and moving scenes, by the ever hovering atmosphere of fatality and death, by the stoic heroism with which these people meet their end, and above all, the sense of the futility of their sacrifice, that *La Condition humaine,* presented as it is with Malraux's habitual dignity, restraint, and force, becomes one of the most powerful and distinctive achievements in contemporary literature.

But the chief interest in Malraux proceeds, not from the stories themselves, but from the special psychology they expound. These revolutionary settings should present broad horizons swept by waves of violent emotions experienced in common by vast multitudes of people. It is therefore surprising to see Malraux concentrating on the study of the lonely man. The fate of these heroes, whose unruly natures are magnets to the steel of revolution, is mainly determined by their own fierce, isolated spirits. When, as in *La Voie royale,* there is no revolution, its heroes—Perken, Claude, and Grabot—prefer the Cambodian forest to their fellow-men.

Malraux's own revolt is against the stupidity and vanity of life, only tolerated, he thinks, by the hypocrite or the dullard. "I do not consider society bad," says Garine in *Les Conquérants,* "I merely find it absurd. Its transformation does not interest me, nor do I deplore the lack of justice. My difficulty arises from the impossibility of giving my adherence to any social form whatever. I am a-social just as I am a-theist, and in the same manner."

A conscientious nihilist, Garine feels that revolution is good in itself, and even though it disgusts him, he looks upon any other condition as something worse. Nor is he inspired by a love for humanity. In fact, he feels nothing but repugnance for the human race. If he prefers the humble and the defeated, it is because he is antagonistic on principle to all victorious causes. His greatest satisfaction comes from having sown in many minds a spirit of revolt similar to his own.

The ambition of these idealists is never directed towards wealth or any form of worldly recognition. Thus, it is not concrete power but the sense of power that Garine craves, and this desire eats into him like a disease. He seeks to affirm himself through acts, the most successful outlet for his energy, and these bring him deliverance and relief. Tchen, who makes of terrorism a sort of mysticism, believes that through assassination he acquires a more complete possession of himself, and invests his solitude with meaning. Kyo, who speaks of communism as man's only dignity, is really striving to establish his own dignity as a congenital nonconformist. In other words, these men are megalomaniacs who, if they have no desire to rule, experience a thrill in imposing their ideas upon the world, or, as Kyo's old father expresses it, "of being, in a world of men, more than men." Fundamentally active natures, they must have a faith for which to die, even though they doubt this faith. In the days of early Rome they would have been ardent Christian martyrs. In fact, it was due to his antipathy to a contemplative life that Tchen, described by his old teacher as "a hawk converted by Saint Francis of Assisi," decided to abandon Christianity. Having no god, these communists dream of being gods themselves; their complete denial of the cosmos, their belief that by their own will they can escape from 'man's fate,' is a dream of omnipotence.

This attitude of superb defiance plunges them into tragic solitude. After committing his first murder, Tchen exclaims: "I feel frightfully alone." Although they believe that the only dignity is that which springs from suffering, this is only gained at the cost of isolation, the worst suffering of all. For their greatest need is love, and of this, life doles out to them the barest modi-

cum. Thwarted in his own attempts to gain affection, Hemmelrich cries out: "Whenever I see people apparently loving one
another, my desire is to smash their faces." Malraux is either indifferent to normal relationships in love or wilfully ignores them.
In the few instances where he introduces love, it proves more of
a torture than a satisfaction. Our first glimpse of May comes
with her confession to her husband that she has been unfaithful
to him that afternoon. As he had previously granted her this
liberty of action, she is surprised to find that he is pained, for
in a strange, despairing way, these two love each other with extraordinary intensity. To Kyo, love represents an uncritical com-
plicity between two human beings, a feeling of permanence,
and a protection against solitude. As he explains it: "He only
loves who loves but does not judge; who loves in face of deteriora-
tion, baseness, treachery; who loves another, in short, as much as
he loves himself; and who would follow this other even to suicide."
Kyo's own love reaches its highest pitch when, knowing his act
may mean death to both, he permits his wife to remain by his
side. Since as communists and revolutionists of one sort or another these people are in constant danger of their lives, their
sense of impending tragedy lends gravity to their loves.

Having pictured man as a solitary captive in a detestable
world, having painted the misery, the ignominy and absurdity of
man's fate, Malraux brings his heroes to the logical conclusion
that death is their only dignity; or, as Kyo's old father sees it:
"Life consists of those fifty years it takes to make a man, fifty
years of sacrifice and will power and so many other things, until,
with childhood and adolescence vanished—in short, when he has
become a man—he is no longer good for anything but to die."
For Malraux sees fatality weighing upon humanity, on the worst
as on the best. What is the liberty of man, he asks in *Le Temps
du mépris,* but the consciousness and the organization of his

fate? Not that these men welcome the thought of dying in itself; thirsting for immortality and the absolute, they are obsessed by the dread of death. In spite of sharing Sancho Panza's philosophy that there is no pain which death will not terminate, their really great love is for life. But of what value would that life be, they ask, for which one would not be willing to die? So, seeking in revolution, not reasons for living—for there are no reasons for living—but reasons for dying, Malraux's heroes die magnificently: Tchen at a revolver muzzle; Kyo from a dose of poison; Katow in a blazing furnace. Kyo's father, too old for action, resorts to opium and is thus enabled to contemplate his end with greater serenity.

In his person, Malraux is constantly defying death. As an archeologist, he has explored the wilds of Afghanistan and Persia, and in his recent search by airplane for the ancient capital of Sheba, he has braved the unknown dangers of the Arabian desert. Perhaps he seeks in lost worlds those values he despairs of ever finding in this. Through space he can soar like a superman. However, it is impossible to imagine him remaining long among the clouds. He has a grim rôle to play among men. Convinced of the impossibility of ameliorating society, he has assumed that other and more desperate task of destroying it. If he chooses to formulate his pessimism in books, he is more than a mere fireside theorist. Before pronouncing a code, he first draws it up from life. Hence, like his heroes, he too has become a communist. Literature for him is simply one gesture of his active existence, or rather, Malraux's literature and Malraux's life are one. To be sure, no writer is more studious of his artistic effects. I feel it is because he believes so strongly in his doctrines that he is careful to render them as graphically as possible. However subversive may be his principles, they are the expression of a fervent idealism. In view of his sincerity, deep human sympathy, and altruism, his attitude of complete negation is not without its tragic sublimity. We listen apprehensively but always with respect to this dynamic younger writer as he sees, weighs, and condemns 'man's fate.'

THE END